JEWS
IN THE
PROTESTANT ESTABLISHMENT

JEWS
IN THE
PROTESTANT ESTABLISHMENT
RICHARD L. ZWEIGENHAFT
G. WILLIAM DOMHOFF

PRAEGER

PRAEGER SPECIAL STUDIES • PRAEGER SCIENTIFIC

Library of Congress Cataloging in Publication Data

Zweigenhaft, Richard L.
  Jews in the Protestant establishment.

  Bibliography: p. 117
  Includes index.
  1. Jews—United States—Social conditions.
  2. Elite (Social sciences)—United States.
  3. Executives—United States. I. Domhoff,
  G. William. II. Title.
  E184.J5Z826   1982 305.5′54′089924073   82-13155
  ISBN 0-03-062607-2
  ISBN 0-03-062606-4 (pbk.)

Published in 1982 by Praeger Publishers
CBS Educational and Professional Publishing
a Division of CBS Inc.
521 Fifth Avenue, New York, New York 10175 U.S.A.

© 1982 by Praeger Publishers

23456789 052 987654321

Printed in the United States of America

Preface

"Oy vey! Jews in the Protestant Establishment?" This was the half-joking, half-serious comment of a friend when we told him of our plans for this book on Jews in the American corporate and social elite. Are there Jews in the Protestant Establishment, he wanted to know, and, even if there are, should it be written about?

Behind his question lies a deeper one: "Is a book about successful Jews ever good for the Jews?" We understand the depth of this concern, and the reasons for it, but we do not think that any scientific book is bad for anyone. This viewpoint was expressed best by Sigmund Freud, who referred to himself as "completely estranged" from religion but in his "essential nature a Jew." In the preface to a Hebrew translation of his classic work on the origins of culture, *Totem and Taboo*, Freud noted that the book "adopts no Jewish standpoint and makes no exceptions in favor of Jewry," but immediately went on to say that "The author hopes, however, that he will be at one with his readers in the conviction that unprejudiced science cannot remain a stranger to the spirit of the new Jewry."

We also write in the belief that only more discussion and information, not silence, will continue the decline in prejudices toward many minority groups that has occurred over the years since the second World War. In the words of sociologist E. Digby Baltzell, whose ideas we are building upon in this book, "the story of the Jews is one of the great untold stories of the twentieth century in America," and the partial telling of that story will further diminish discrimination, not feed it.

As longtime friends whose backgrounds and styles complement each other—one is lefthanded, the other righthanded; one is adversarial, the other conciliatory; one a social psychologist, the other a political sociologist; one of Jewish background, the other not—it was our expectation that this book would be a pleasure to research and write. This has proved to be the case. We can only hope that people will find it half as informative and enjoyable to read as we have found it to write.

Our thanks to all those corporate directors who shared their time, experiences, and observations with us, and did so in a gracious and candid manner. Many of them are quoted by name throughout our narrative, but when they requested it, or when we thought it suitable, we have quoted them anonymously. Similarly, we thank our various friends in major cities around the country who provided bed, breakfast, and directions downtown.

We also would like to thank the following people for their thoughtful and helpful comments on an earlier version of the manuscript: E. Digby Baltzell, Leonard Dinnerstein, Calvin S. Hall, Jacqueline Ludel, Cynthia R. Margolin, Kim McQuaid, Lynne Miller, Claire Morse, Thomas Pettigrew, Larry Simon, Michael Useem, and Chaim I. Waxman. Our deepest gratitude, too, to Elizabeth Hunt for her careful typing of the manuscript.

Most of all we'd like to express our thanks to Irene and Twigs Zweigenhaft for lovingly transmitting so many invaluable components of Jewish culture to the senior author, and for being such understanding and supportive parents. The book is dedicated to Lisa Young, wife of the senior author and former research assistant of the junior author, with love for her companionship, appreciation for her warmth, and admiration for her artistic talents.

Table of Contents

JEWS
IN THE
PROTESTANT ESTABLISHMENT

Chapter 1

At the Top
of
the Melting Pot

This book on Jews in the corporate and social elites has a dual purpose. The first is to understand if and how these elites preserve their privileged position through the assimilation of people of a minority religious background who have acquired their wealth relatively recently. At the same time, the book has a second purpose: to understand these new members of the upper class themselves and the way their arrival in the corporate and social elites affects their own experience and identity as Jews. The first, then, is a sociological focus on the class system in America. The second is on the social psychology of identity.

The person who has approached these issues most thoughtfully has been E. Digby Baltzell, a sociologist whose books on *Philadelphia Gentlemen* (1958) and *The Protestant Establishment* (1964) have been major contributions to understanding the American upper class. We will examine Baltzell's hypotheses to see how effectively they account for the patterns of Jewish assimilation into the upper class during the 18 years since the publication of *The Protestant Establishment*.

Baltzell believes that the maintenance of the upper class as a source of societal authority and stability critically depends upon the assimilation of new members who are economically successful, whatever their race, creed or color. If this assimilation takes place, then the upper class will continue to be a "ruling class" or "establishment": "The upper class, in other words, will be a ruling class, or as I should prefer to say, its leaders will form an establishment." Baltzell goes on to say that "In a free society, while an establishment will always be dominated by upper-class members, it also must be constantly rejuvenated by members of the elite who are in the process of acquiring upper-class status" (1964: 8).

It is Baltzell's belief that the establishment in America is losing power because it is no longer assimilating new members who are of minority backgrounds, and particularly those of Jewish backgrounds. It is for this reason that he chastises the establishment as a "Protestant Establishment," and urges it to mend its discriminatory ways.

In this book we examine Baltzell's thesis of a declining establishment by determining the degree to which economically successful Jews have become part of the corporate and social elites. In so doing, we will be able to see if the assimilatory processes Baltzell describes have, in fact, failed for this particular minority group.

Baltzell also has considered the effect of arriving in the upper class on the individual's self-concept. He suggested that the class structure is pyramidal, and that within the broader society there are three major class divisions (upper, middle, and lower) as well as three major religious groupings (Protestant, Catholic, and Jew). As people "move up" in class within each of the three religious communities, they acculturate but do not move outside the broad boundaries of their religion.

But according to Baltzell, things are qualitatively different at the very top of the class hierarchy. At that level, what Baltzell refers to as "the overwhelming factor of class" becomes more important than religion. As Baltzell puts it (1964: 63), "while there are upper-, middle-, and lower-class levels *within the Protestant, Catholic, and Jewish communities*, there are Protestants, Catholics, and Jews *within the elite*." Baltzell's hypothesis suggests, therefore, that Jews who do reach the top of the class hierarchy will be less likely to emphasize religion and more likely to emphasize class in the way they think of themselves, and in the way they present themselves.

In our investigation, we have employed several different methods to determine the usefulness of Baltzell's framework. The primary one has been semistructured personal interviews with 30 Jews who sit on the boards of directors of major American corporations. These interviews, conducted over a 12-month period and ranging in length from 45 minutes to two and a half hours, included questions about their routes to the corporate boards, their experiences and perceptions as Jews in the corporate world, and their treatment by the most prestigious social clubs in their cities. The interviews also included questions about their grandparents, parents, and children, bar mitzvahs, synagogue attendance, intermarriages, and feelings about Israel.

These interviews were supplemented by analyses of what these Jews, and thousands of other Jews (some of whom were corporate directors, and some of whom were not) do and do not put in published biographical sources like *Who's Who in America*. Examining the way they presented themselves in these public resource books allowed us to estimate their public Jewish identity. Some identify strongly enough to reveal directly that they are Jewish; others include memberships in Jewish organizations (such as B'nai B'rith, or the American Jewish Committee); others include membership in Jewish clubs (like the Harmonie Club of New York); and others give no indication whatsoever of being Jewish.

The data from the interviews, and from published biographical sources, have been supplemented by additional published material and various membership lists we have been able to obtain. All of these materials were analyzed using empirical techniques that have been developed by social psychologists and by political sociologists in the field that has come to be referred to as "power structure research" (see Domhoff, 1980).

Although our systematic data reveal quite clearly the general picture of Jewish acceptance into the Protestant Establishment, it does not capture the more subtle nuances of assimilation that came through in the interviews, particularly in the recounting of family histories. We, therefore, have attempted to straddle two worlds, the first drawing on quantitative studies that we and others have completed, and the second drawing on the telling anecdote as gleaned in our interviews. Such an attempt carries the risk of sounding overly impressionistic, but our account is nonetheless based on all the available studies that have been produced by social scientists. We are hopeful that our approach will make the book accessible and enjoyable to students and interested laymen as well as more enriching to fellow social scientists.

Before examining Baltzell's hypotheses in further detail, it is necessary to explain what we mean by the terms "corporate elite" and "social elite," and what we mean by the term "Jewish." Although these terms are used frequently in everyday discourse, none has been defined in a manner that is accepted universally, and it is therefore necessary to explain what we mean by them.

THE CORPORATE ELITE

Increasingly, wealth in America is under corporate control. In *The Power Elite*, first published in 1956, C. Wright Mills argued that the economic elite had become a corporate elite. We find his argument even more true today:

> In realizing the power of property and in acquiring instruments for its protection, the very rich have become involved, and now they are deeply entrenched, in the higher corporate world of the twentieth-century American economy. Not great fortunes, but great corporations are the

important units of wealth, to which individuals of property are variously
attached. The corporation is the source of wealth, and the basis of the
continued power and privilege of wealth. All the men and the families of
great wealth are now identified with large corporations in which their
property is seated (Mills, 1956: 116).

Because of the role corporations play in creating and maintaining
wealth in America, we have used directorships on the top corporations
listed by *Fortune* magazine as our index of membership in the economic or
corporate elite. This is not to deny that there are some people with
immense personal fortunes who are not involved as directors in corporate America; rather it is to assert that directing a major American
corporation is a meaningful indicator that one is a member of a corpora-
tized economic elite. In general, we have used the entire 1,300 corporations included on *Fortune's* annual list (the top 500 industrials, the
second 500 industrials, and the top 50 commercial banks, life insurance
companies, diversified financial companies, retail merchandising companies, transportation companies, and utilities), but we have noted at
what level an individual is involved in the corporate world. For example,
consider two successful businessmen of Jewish backgrounds: George
Szabad, who sits on the board of Burndy Corporation (the 700th largest
industrial corporation in America in 1981) and Joseph F. Cullman 3rd,
who sits on the boards of Ford (#6), Philip Morris (#46), and Levi Strauss
(#138). Both are part of the corporate elite, but Cullman's involvement
is much closer to the center of economic power in America.

THE SOCIAL ELITE

The social elite consists of those people who are generally acknowledged
by society editors and social chroniclers to be part of high society or
"the upper crust." It is the top status group in a society (e.g., Kahl, 1959).
Baltzell provides a useful definition when he says that the core of the
social elite is "a community of upper-class families whose members are
born to positions of high prestige and assured dignity because their
ancestors have been leaders (elite members) for one generation or more"
(Baltzell, 1964: 7). His study of the social elite, or upper class, in Philadelphia used attendance at private secondary schools, membership in
exclusive gentlemen's clubs, attendance at exclusive summer resorts,
and listing in a high-society address and telephone book called *The Social
Register* as his indicators of inclusion within this elite. Building on the
work of Baltzell, Domhoff (1970: 11–17) queried society page editors in
dozens of large cities and conducted a statistical study of *Who's Who in*

America entries to extend these indicators to include 40 social clubs and 37 prep schools throughout the country. It is this list of clubs and schools that we have used as our "operational definition" of the social elite, and we will use the terms "social elite" and "upper class" interchangeably to describe it.

The key issue for Baltzell, and for much of the research on class and power in America, has been the degree of overlap between the corporate and social elites. Baltzell found considerable overlap between the two elites for 1890 to 1940 in his detailed history of Philadelphia and provided preliminary evidence for several other cities as well. Mills (1956), Domhoff (1967, 1970), Dye (1976), and others have extended this work to other cities and to the nation as a whole. We have examined in detail the extent to which Jews who have become part of America's corporate elite also have become members of the social elite.

WHO IS JEWISH?

The discussion so far has proceeded as if it is entirely clear what it means when a person is described as "Jewish." In fact, anthropologist Melville Herskovitz (1974: 473) has written that "of all human groupings, there is none wherein the problem of definition has proved to be more difficult than for the Jews." Given considerable disagreement as to the meaning of this term, it is necessary to discuss it in some detail before any systematic inquiry can occur.

There are at least four different ways that can be used to identify "Jewishness." The most traditional definition is based on the body of Jewish religious law called the "halacha," which states that a person is Jewish if born to a Jewish mother, or if he or she has followed a prescribed set of procedures to convert to Judaism. According to this definition, those who lose their faith, those who never had any faith, and even those who find another faith are still considered Jews if their mothers were Jewish. Thus, Bob Dylan, who was born as Robert Zimmerman to Jewish parents, but who became a born-again Christian in the late 1970s, would be considered Jewish. Or, to cite another example, Robert Moses, lionized in Robert Caro's Pulitzer Prize winning book, *The Power Broker*, as "the shaper of the greatest city in the world" (1974: 19), would be considered Jewish because his mother was Jewish, even though he insisted he was not, sent his daughters to an Episcopalian school, and threatened to sue the *Jewish Encyclopedia* if it included his biography.

A second way to define Jewishness is not based on matters of birth, or conversion, but on matters of conviction. According to this definition, people are Jewish if they view themselves as being Jewish. This would include those whose mothers were Jewish and who view themselves as being Jewish (not Bob Dylan); those who have converted (like baseball star Rod Carew and entertainer Sammy Davis, Jr.); and those whose fathers were Jewish and who view themselves as being Jewish. The "viewing oneself" as Jewish, that is, the inclusion of Jewishness as part of one's identity, may occur for various reasons. It may be spiritual; it may be cultural; or it may be a way of honoring or identifying with one's parents. For some, it may be political. In an article entitled, "Am I a Jew? A Radical's Search for an Answer," Peggy Dennis, a life-long member of the Communist Party who had been raised an atheist, wrote:

> I still have never been inside a synagogue. I still do not like matzos. I still have no ethnic affinity with Israel and am more critical than ever of the Israeli Government, Jewish though it may be. I now know less Yiddish than I did as a child. I know no more of Yiddish literature, culture, or history than I ever did. I still am not clear why I am, but I know I am a Jew.
>
> Eugene Debs wrote, defining his personal and social credo: "While there is a lower class, I am in it. While there is a criminal element, I am of it. While there is a soul in prison, I am not free." I guess the answer to my confusion over my ethnicity lies in adding one further phrase to Debs's words: While anti-Semitism and ethnic discrimination exist anywhere, I am a Jew (Dennis, 1980: 48).

A third way to define Jewishness is based on an ancestral tabulation, according to which one who has one Jewish parent is "half-Jewish," one who has one Jewish grandparent is "one-fourth" Jewish, and so on. Such an attempt to define Jewishness in racial, ancestral terms was employed by the Nazis. As social psychologist Simon Herman (1977: 81) points out, this approach is riddled with contradiction and absurdities: "The Nazi regime in its Nuremburg laws adopted a sweeping definition embracing even those who were no longer in the Jewish fold but who had a Jewish grandparent. On the other hand, an individual of 'pure Aryan' ancestry who had converted to Judaism—and who was accordingly regarded as Jewish by Jews—was not classified as a Jew under the Nuremburg laws."

Similar definitions have been used by anti-Semitic social clubs in the United States. C. Douglas Dillon, a centimillionaire Episcopalian of high social standing (who took his mother's name of Dillon rather than his father's Old-World name of Lapowski), was kept on the waiting list at the Chevy Chase Club, outside of Washington, D.C., because he was one-fourth Jewish. Barry Goldwater, another Episcopalian, but worth only 2 or 3 million, was allegedly barred from playing a round of golf at the same club. He wryly suggested that he be allowed to play nine holes, not the customary 18, because he was only "half Jewish" (Baltzell, 1964: 84–86).

A fourth definition of Jewishness, somewhat similar to the second definition above, is based on membership in Jewish institutions such as synagogues or Jewish clubs. Such membership not only implies that one's self-identity includes being Jewish, but it also implies some willingness for Jewish affiliations to be part of one's public identity. As Herman (1977: 36) says: "In the Diaspora religious institutions such as the synagogue serve more than just a religious function in the Jewish community and affiliation with them is often an expression of Jewish identification rather than of religiosity."

In order to probe social psychological questions related to identity, we have drawn primarily, but not exclusively, on the fourth definition— membership in one or more Jewish organizations. Using such membership as an operational definition of who is Jewish has allowed us to identify a set of individuals in the national corporate and social elites that we know to be Jewish. In addition, as we will describe in detail in our final chapter, this approach has allowed us to develop a scale with which we have been able to assess the way people do, or do not, present themselves publicly as Jews.

We have not, however, depended on this fourth definition exclusively. When someone's parents were Jewish but he or she has not joined any Jewish organizations, we believe that this also says something concerning that person's sense of identity that may be helpful in understanding the relative importance of class and ethnic identity at the top of the social ladder. To say, for example, that Walter Lippman was born to wealthy and well-assimilated Jewish parents but would not join any Jewish organizations, or even speak before any Jewish groups, and that he refused to accept an award from the Jewish Academy of Arts and Sciences, is to say something about his rejection of Jewishness in his personal identity (Steel, 1980).

ANTI-SEMITISM AT THE TOP

In the fall of 1974, General George S. Brown, the Chairman of the Joint Chiefs of Staff at the time, made headlines in newspapers across the country by saying to a Duke University audience that American Jews "own, you know, the banks in this country, the newpapers, you just look at where the Jewish money is in this country" (The Washington Post, 1974a: A1). General Brown's ill-fated remark, captured on tape by a Duke University law student, was met by a barrage of protest. Editorial writers lambasted the general for his ignorance and for his anti-Semitism. As The

New York Times, 1974b: 46) put it: "the general's opinions ... can only be read as a perpetuation of the myths on which bigotry has fed for centuries, here and abroad." Jewish leaders issued shocked and angry statements. Senator William Proxmire, a member of the Senate Banking Committee, pointed out that "there is probably no industry in this country that has more consistently and cruelly rejected Jews from positions of power and influence than commercial banking" (*The Washington Post*, 1974b: A8). Proxmire, along with other members of Congress, called for Brown's dismissal. Brown acknowledged that his comments were "unfortunate," "ill-considered," "unfounded," and "all too casual," but did not directly retract his statement (*The New York Times*, 1974a: 1). A few weeks later, he sheepishly informed the members of the Comstock Club, a business-man's group in Sacramento, "I have learned a good deal about the corpo-rate structure of banks and newspapers" (*The Washington Post*, 1974c: A5). President Ford was not happy about General Brown's comments, but he did not dismiss him.

Unfortunately, General Brown's views were not notably atypical. When survey researchers asked a random sample of Americans whether or not they agreed with Brown's claim that Jews "own the banks and newspapers in this country," one in every five said yes. Moreover, systematic questionnaire studies of anti-Semitic stereotypes reveal that fully one-third of Americans harbor enough prejudices about the alleged clannishness or dishonesty or greed of Jews to be classified as anti-Semites (Quinley and Glock, 1979: 9, 185).

We think it is necessary to "look at where the Jewish money is in this country," but not for the same reasons that apparently were behind Brown's claim. In addition to the obvious need to continue to correct his mistaken and dangerous views (especially since so many Americans share them), we believe that by looking at where Jews have been successful economically, and where they have not, we can learn valuable lessons about the patterns of interaction between wealthy gentiles and wealthy Jews in America. Going beyond questions of wealth, we also want to look at where Jews have been accepted or excluded socially, and the way such acceptance or exclusion affects economic success and religious identity. It is by focusing on this interaction that we can gain insight into the relationship between class and religion in America.

In order to understand the present-day relationships between upper-class gentiles and Jews in America, however, it is necessary to take a brief detour into history. Different groups of Jews came to America in varying numbers at different times, and this fact had pro-found influence on gentile-Jewish relations and, for that matter, on relationships among Jews.

JEWISH IMMIGRATION TO AMERICA

There have been three major waves of Jewish immigration to America, and each has led to a different relationship between Jews and the predominantly gentile upper class.

The earliest Jewish settlers were Sephardic Jews, descendants of Jews who had been expelled from Spain and Portugal in the fifteenth century. They arrived by accident in 1654 when their ship, bound from Brazil to the Netherlands, was captured by Spanish pirates. The pirate ship was, in turn, taken by a French-commissioned privateer that was on its way to New Amsterdam, the Dutch colony in the New World, where it finally unloaded its 23 Jewish passengers after delicate negotiations between local authorities and the ship's captain over payment for their "passage" (Birmingham, 1971: 53–59).

Over 100 years later, when the first census was conducted in 1790, there were about 2,000 Jews living in American colonies (Baltzell, 1964: 55; Handlin, 1954). Because there were so few of them, and because they were so widely dispersed throughout the colonies, they had a great deal of interaction with non-Jews. They were, for the most part, successful merchants, and are described by Manners (1972: 63) in the following way:

> By combining a proud adherence to their faith, an ineluctable gift for achieving affluence and an impressively grand manner, the Sephardim were first among equals in the new democracy for which they had fought in the Revolutionary War. (Of course a few were loyal to King George III, and they packed up and went to England to live among the British upper class, where it was supposed they were happier with their own kind.) They were the elite, among the founders of such Establishment institutions as the New York Stock Exchange, Columbia University, New York University, the American Medical Association, and the Boston Athenaeum.

Despite their "proud adherence to their faith," there was among the Sephardic Jews a high frequency of intermarriage with gentiles and extensive assimilation. This was caused in part by the shortage of Jewish females, and in part by the absence of rabbis. Baltzell (1964: 55) writes that "This, then, was the classic period of aristocratic assimilation, and even today there are leading families within the old-stock and Protestant upper class, some of whose ancestors were prominent Jews during the Colonial period." Perhaps a typical example would be the marriage in 1923 of Godrey S. Rockefeller, a nephew of the original John D. Rockefeller and an important financial leader in his own right, to Helen Gratz, a descendant of a distinguished Sephardic Jewish family that had converted to Episcopalianism early in the nineteenth century (Birmingham, 1971: 181).

The second major wave of Jewish immigration, in the mid-nineteenth century, brought German Jews to every section of America. They came in numbers large enough to create Jewish communities and, unlike their Sephardic predecessors, they came with rabbis. As of 1880, every state had a Jewish community, though Jews were not yet clustered in urban areas. In 1880, for example, New York City's population was only 3 percent Jewish (Baltzell, 1964: 56). These German Jews were typically middle-class entrepreneurs. Whatever their occupation in the "old country" (many were foreign traders and stockbrokers), most had to start from scratch when they came to America. Birmingham (1967) and Supple (1957) have recounted the way in which many Jewish immigrants of this era (including Joseph Seligman, Simon and Meyer Guggenheim, and Henry Lehman) started as peddlers. By the 1870s, a number of these immigrants had become extremely wealthy. In fact, historian John Higham (1975: 144) tells us that, "Proportionally speaking, in no other immigrant group have so many men ever risen so rapidly from rags to riches."

Like the Sephardim who preceded them, the wealthiest German Jews were accepted in the most prestigious clubs, and many interacted with and were entertained socially by "the best" gentile society. Indeed, many Jews were influential in founding the very clubs that helped set the upper class apart from the rest of society. For example, sugar merchant Moses Lazarus, a descendant of Sephardic Jews, was a founder of New York's Knickerbocker Club in 1871, and investment banker Joseph Seligman helped found the Union League in 1863. Baltzell (1964: 56) writes: "Even as late as the 1870s, when young Louis D. Brandeis was welcomed into the best Boston society, Jews still belonged to the best clubs in many cities, and a leading society journal could feature the news of a fashionable 'Hebrew Wedding' in New York's Orthodox Thirty-fourth Street Synagogue."

During this period of German-Jewish immigration, there developed what could be considered a national Jewish upper class that had considerable overlap with the non-Jewish social elite. Many members of this group (such as the Guggenheims, Lehmans, Schiffs, Seligmans, and Warburgs) ended up living in New York and have been popularized in Birmingham's *Our Crowd* (1967). But influential and wealthy German Jews lived outside New York as well and were, for the most part, accepted into the predominantly gentile upper class society. There were, for example, "the Gimbels and Brentanos in Vincennes, Indiana; Adolph Gluck of Dodge City, Kansas; the Rosenwalds of Chicago; the Rosewaters of Omaha, Nebraska; the Michaelsons of Virginia City, Nevada; the Spiegelbergs of Santa Fe, New Mexico; the Seasongoods of Cincinnati, Ohio . . ." (Manners, 1972: 65). These Jewish immigrants wanted to be more like other Americans and less like immigrants and made vigorous efforts to assimilate into American culture. Some were "assimilated completely through marriage or conversion and others through membership in exclusive clubs and associations" (Baltzell, 1964: 58).

For the most part, then, Jews were not discriminated against during this period; nonetheless, the images of Jews held by many people were not wholly favorable. Higham (1975: 139) points out the important distinction between behavior and attitudes: "The image of Scotsmen as stiff-necked and penurious and the image of Englishmen as snobs have not handicapped members of either of these groups in America. Similarly, the Jews in early-nineteenth-century America got along very well with their non-Jewish neighbors although American conceptions of Jews in the abstract at no time lacked the unfavorable elements embedded in European tradition."

In the 1880s, Eastern European Jews began to arrive in America in great numbers, and the comfortable relationship between upper-class Jews and gentiles changed. Between 1881 and the passage of the American Immigration Act in 1924, more than two and a half million Jews came to the United States from Russia alone; this was the largest exodus of Jews "since the one from Egypt" (Birmingham, 1967: 289). By 1907, about 90,000 Jews, mostly from Russia and Poland, were arriving in New York City every year (Manners, 1972: 51). By 1930, there were 4 million American Jews, and 80 percent of them were of Eastern-European origins. Unlike the Sephardic and German Jews, this third wave of Jewish immigrants consisted primarily of wage workers. They were, in Birmingham's words (1967: 289; see also Rischin, 1962: 94): "ragged, dirt-poor, culturally energetic, toughened by years of torment, idealistic, and socialistic." They had little in common with those Jews who had preceded them except their shared religion, and even that was not without significant differences. As Nathan Glazer and Daniel Moynihan (1963: 139) point out in Beyond the Melting Pot, "In practice, tone, and theology, the Reform Judaism of the German Jews diverged from the Orthodoxy of the immigrants as much as the beliefs and practices of Southern Baptists differ from those of New England Unitarians." The heavy influx of lower-class Jews, densely settled in urban areas along the East coast, was accompanied by increasingly frequent episodes of anti-Semitism. Indeed anti-Semitism more than anything else ultimately may have brought the Jews of different backgrounds closer together (Rollins, 1973; Steinberg, 1981: 55).

The first widely publicized anti-Semitic incident actually occurred in 1877, a few years before the heavy influx of Eastern European Jews began, when Joseph Seligman was refused accommodation at the Grand Union Hotel in Saratoga. Saratoga was, at that time, "the queen of American resorts," and the Grand Union Hotel was by far the most elegant hotel in Saratoga; it was the kind of place to which people took their valets, personal maids, laundresses, and even chefs, and settled in for a long stay (Birmingham, 1967: 143). When Seligman was informed that the hotel had adopted a new policy that did not allow it to accept "Israelites," he wrote a scathing letter to the owner of the hotel and released it to the newspapers. The matter received a great deal of coverage in the press, with many expressing shock and outrage that this could happen in America. But happen it did in Saratoga, and it soon began to happen elsewhere. Other resorts asserted their exclusivity by advertising "No Jews Accepted," "Hebrews Need Not Apply," or "Hebrews Will Knock Vainly for Admission" (Birmingham, 1967: 147; Manners, 1972: 58; Rischin, 1962: 261).

The exclusion of Jews from resorts was followed by their exclusion from certain social clubs. In 1893, the Union League Club of New York refused to admit Theodore Seligman, the son of one of the club's founders (and the nephew of Joseph), even though his membership was staunchly supported by such respected members as Joseph Choate and Elihu Root. Higham (1975: 151) informs us that by the turn of the century "Jewish penetration into the most elite circles in the East had become almost impossibly difficult." And by 1920, as public a figure as Henry Ford was embarking on a viciously anti-Semitic campaign in which he and his newspaper, the Dearborn *Independent*, argued that Jews or their gentile "fronts" (including former President William H. Taft) controlled every aspect of American life (Manners, 1972: 298).

In 1922, A. A. Lowell, the president of Harvard, urged the university to adopt a quota system to solve "the Jewish problem." A similar stance by the president of Columbia University, Nicholas Murray Butler, cut the percentage of Jews at Columbia from 40 percent to 20 percent within two years (Baltzell, 1964: 210–211; Synnott, 1979: 14–17). And if Harvard and Columbia used quotas, would other schools be far behind? Wechsler (1977: 162) reports that during the 1920s many medical and other professional schools joined with a growing number of undergraduate colleges in restricting access to Jewish students, either directly or indirectly through "geographical quotas." Most of these barriers would not come down until after World War II.

The rather abrupt appearance of overt anti-Semitism at just about the same time when tens of thousands of Eastern European Jews arrived in America led to a hostile reception for the new immigrants by many established American Jews. As Esther Panitz (1963: 105) writes, "With but few exceptions, from 1870 to 1890, America's representative Jews were not eager to welcome their kin from abroad." She goes on (1963: 118):

> Though American Jews had been subjected to instances of anti-Semitic bias, they were still free to attempt to scale the ladder of economic and social acceptability. But they were most fearful lest the alien customs and manners of their immigrant relatives imperil their ascent. Numerous studies have by now quoted oft-repeated judgments by America's established Jewry, concerning the allegedly uncivilized modes of life deemed endemic to their East-European kin.

There were some elite social clubs for German Jews prior to the onset of overt anti-Semitism in the 1880s. For example, New York's Harmonie Club, founded in 1852, was one of the oldest social clubs in the city. But when upper-class German Jews were no longer accepted in upper-class gentile social clubs, they formed their own fashionable clubs—and did not accept Eastern European Jews. In fact, their efforts at exclusion involved more than just clubs. They created their own neighborhoods, their own summer resorts, and their own Reform synagogues as well.

Although many of these institutions maintained their exclusion of Eastern European Jews well into the 1930s, by the beginning of World War II most had absorbed Jews of Eastern European origin who had become rich and influential. In an article published early in 1946, Solomon Bloom (1946: 7) claimed a new phase had been reached in the relationship between Eastern and Western Jews.

> The clash between Eastern and Western Jews has lost its former intensity. The events of the last decade, the fear of a common danger, have brought about a strong rapprochement. The Eastern Jew is losing his self-consciousness and his sense of neglect, the Western is shedding his traditional attitude of exclusiveness. East and West meet, and they are perforce becoming one. Slowly.

Although comments by such public figures as General Brown (and, a few years later, Billy Carter) underscore the general finding of survey researchers that many Americans continue to hold prejudicial attitudes about Jews, there has been a decline in these attitudes, and anti-Semitic behavior is not as virulent and open as it was in the 1920s, 1930s, and early 1940s (Pettigrew, 1966). There once again seems to be more behavioral tolerance and social interaction. Figures on intermarriage also suggest a decline in anti-Semitism. One study showed that among the generation of Jews that married between 1966 and 1972, the number who married out of the faith had climbed to 32 percent from a figure that had been below 10 percent only 25 years earlier (Cohen, S. M., 1979: 7; Steinberg, 1981: 69). The *National Jewish Population Study*, published by the Council of Jewish Federations and Welfare Funds, estimated that the intermarriage rate was 29.1 percent in 1965 and had risen to 48.1 percent by 1972 (Waxman, 1981: 8).

Perhaps America is once again becoming a "melting pot" as far as Jews are concerned. This possibility leads us directly to the sociological notion of a "triple" or "multiple" melting pot, thereby providing a starting point for our look at the corporate and social elites in America.

At the Top of the Melting Pot

The concept of the "melting pot" was applied to American society as early as 1782 when J. Hector St. John de Crèvecoeur wrote of this country that "here individuals of all nations are melted into a new race of men" (Gordon, 1964: 114). In 1909, Israel Zangwell's play entitled "The Melting Pot" was performed in New York, Chicago, and Washington. The play was a smash hit, and the term "melting pot" became a regular part of the American vocabulary.

The argument that American culture was a melting pot presumed that, over time, racial, religious and cultural differences would blend into one unique American culture, drawing from all groups, but distinguished primarily by no particular one of them. As sociologist Ruby Jo Reeves Kennedy (1944: 331) put it:

America has long been described as a great and bottomless melting-pot into which have been thrown peoples from all parts of the world. Boiling and seething there together, they will, it is believed, ultimately lose all distinguishable marks of their diverse backgrounds; and some fine day American society will become one homogeneous group—a single amalgam blended of the many and varied types brought to our shores by the great waves of immigration of the past century.

Kennedy set out, in the early 1940s, to investigate this hypothesis. Using intermarriage as both "the surest means of assimilation and the most infallible index of its occurrence" (1944: 331), she attempted to gauge the degree to which Americans had, over time, relinquished the distinguishable characteristics of their varied backgrounds. She investigated the records of 8,044 marriages in New Haven, Connecticut, over a 70-year period, looking in depth at those which occurred in 1870, 1900, 1930, and 1940. The records she studied included seven "white ethnic" groups: Italians, Irish, Jews, British-Americans, Germans, Poles, and Scandinavians.

Kennedy's major finding was that there was a clear loosening of "strict endogamy" (in-marriage) among the various groups, but a persistence of "religious endogamy." Thus, to cite one example, the rate of in-marriage for the Irish-Americans dropped from 93 percent in 1870, to 75 percent in 1900, to 74 percent in 1930, and to 45 percent in 1940, but those who married out of the group tended to marry other Catholics. Over the 70 years, the in-marriage rate for all the groups combined dropped from 91 percent in 1870 to 64 percent in 1940. When the data were analyzed along religious rather than ethnic lines, however, the rate of in-marriage for Protestants was 80 percent by 1940, the rate for Catholics was 84 percent, and the rate for Jews was 94 percent. In a subsequent article that extended the data to 1950, Kennedy (1952) found continuing patterns of religious endogamy. Kennedy therefore rejected the "single-melting-pot" idea, and instead proposed the "triple-melting-pot," in which a separate melting pot was proposed for each of the three major religious groups. "Cultural lines may fade," wrote Kennedy, "but religious barriers are holding fast" (1944: 332–334).

In his book *Protestant-Catholic-Jew* (1955, revised 1960), Will Herberg elaborated on Kennedy's theory of the triple-melting-pot, demonstrating how the process of ethnic and cultural integration took place over the generations within each of these three religious communities. Herberg argued that within each of the three communities what emerges is a "new man," but not one who combines all ethnic ingredients in one transcendent and indistinguishable blend. Rather each "new man"—the Protestant, the Catholic, and the Jew—is based primarily on a "national type" that is rooted in the story of the *Mayflower* and such figures as Davy Crockett, George Washington, and Abraham Lincoln. Everyone has to take on the Anglo-Saxon image in some shape or form. "Our cultural assimilation," argued Herberg (1960: 21), "has taken place not in a melting pot, but rather in a 'transmuting pot' in which all ingredients have been transformed and assimilated to an idealized 'Anglo-Saxon' model."

Milton Gordon, in his *Assimilation in American Life* (1964), concludes that there may be more than one, or even three, melting pots. Certain ethnic subsocieties may not be allowed to melt in (as with some racial groups), or they may choose to remain ethnically separate (as with Hasidic Jews). These various groups of people, according to Gordon, over time become culturally similar but structurally separate. He suggests that the entire picture may be referred to as a "multiple melting pot," or as "structural pluralism."

In recent years, questions have been raised about the melting pot theory because of the possibility that it gives too much prominence to ethnicity and not enough to class (e.g., Steinberg, 1981). Reacting against the notion that the "ethnics" are going to be around for a long time to come, this view suggests that class may be as important at other levels of society as Baltzell thinks it is at the upper one. Whatever the eventual outcome of this argument, which will be decided by future data on marriage and interaction patterns, our concerns are essentially above the fray. Our concern is not with class in general, but with class at the top. For our purposes, it will be enough to see if class forces outweigh ethnic and religious forces for a group of people who make up less than 0.5 percent of the social ladder.

In this book, then, we will be studying the upper class and testing the idea that it is becoming weaker by seeing if the assimilatory process has failed in the case of Jews. At the same time, we will examine the effects of upper-class assimilation on Jews. We begin in the second chapter with a consideration of those Jews who have become a part of the American corporate elite. We will examine their presence in the highest corporate circles, looking specifically at the extent to which they are represented and the routes they have, and have not, taken to get there.

In Chapter 3, we will turn to the question of whether the Jews who enter the corporate elite also become part of the social elite. We will look specifically at elite social clubs, schools, and cultural boards to see whether or not the same pattern of overlap between members of the corporate elite and members of the social elite found by Baltzell (1964), Mills (1956), Dye (1976), and others applies to Jews as well as gentiles.

In Chapter 4, our research on Jews in the South will provide an opportunity to examine this process in smaller cities, and in a region sometimes thought to have been the most hospitable to Jews in America. If, in fact, the South has been the region most friendly to Jews, then it follows that it should be the place that has given upper-class assimilation the best chance to occur.

Finally, in Chapter 5 we will look at the question of identity. We will use our interviews, and a scale of public Jewish identity that we have applied to published biographical sourcebooks, such as *Who's Who in America*, to examine Baltzell's hypothesis that at the top of the class hierarchy, class is more salient to identity than is religion. We will explore personal experiences (such as encountering anti-Semitism, intermarriage, and synagogue attendance) and personal feelings about being Jewish. This chapter will include a section on personal and political involvement with Israel. We will conclude the chapter by returning to Baltzell's speculation that the Protestant Establishment has weakened itself by not assimilating Jews into its ranks.

Chapter 2

Jews
in
the Corporate Elite

INTRODUCTION: THE CORPORATE COMMUNITY

Just 200 years ago, at the time of the founding of the Republic, corporations were viewed as extremely dangerous entities. Not only were they seen as instruments of oppression, according to eighteenth-century wisdom, but they were thought to inhibit the individual initiative from which all true enterprise presumably springs. So strong were these concerns that when the Founding Fathers met to write a new Constitution they prohibited the federal government from chartering corporations.

But the separate states still had the right to permit corporations, and corporations soon began to appear. By 1835, there were enough of them that just keeping them within limited bounds became a major preoccupation of politicians and jurists alike. "For the next fifty years," writes A. A. Berle, Jr., a corporate lawyer as well as a leading scholar on the modern corporation, "our great-grandfathers used every known legal means to keep a corporation to a single defined and manageable task" (1964: 93). For a time they succeeded, but the rise of great railroad corporations in the second half of the century signaled the wave of the future.

It was the merger movement at the turn of the twentieth century that changed rural and small-business America into a corporate America. Between 1898 and 1904, as the underlying tensions generated by the growth of nationwide markets came to a head, dozens of giant corporations suddenly were created through a combination of mergers, reorganizations, and internal growth, dwarfing all but a few of the dominant corporations, trusts, and partnerships of the old order. Fully half of the 100 largest industrial corporations that existed in 1899 were created in that year. In 1901, 23 new corporations joined the top 100 for the first time—13 by merger, 5 by a combination of merger and reorganization, and 5 by internal growth (Bunting, 1972: 37–39). Corporate America had arrived, and with minor fluctuations over the decades, it has grown to the point where a few hundred industrial firms and a few dozen firms in each of the other economic sectors dominate the entire economy.

As corporations merged and grew in size, their owners, managers, and financial backers formed themselves into a corporate community whose social bonds include common stock ownership, joint corporate ventures, marketing agreements, shared bankers and legal advisers, and, most visibly, an arrangement called "interlocking directors" (people who are on the board of directors of two or more corporations). Because of the relative ease with which interlocking directorships can be identified, they became the "tracer" elements through which social analysts began to chart the nature and shape of the corporate community, revealing a dense network with banks at the center and held together by a relative handful of directors. With minor exceptions, this network has remained relatively unchanged in its basic outlines since the 1920s (Bunting, 1976, 1977; Mizruchi, 1982; Roy, 1980).

Although the core of the corporate community is composed of companies ranked as the largest in their areas by *Fortune* magazine, there are other elements within it. These include a score of New York investment banking firms, which provide financial advice and help corporations raise money through stocks and bonds; several large law firms in every major city that render essential legal services; the "big eight" accounting firms; the advertising agencies on Madison Avenue; the trade associations in Washington; and the policy-discussion groups and think tanks. All are geared to serve the interests of the major banks and corporations.

Not everyone is equal when it comes to leadership within this corporate community that easily includes between 15,000 and 20,000 members in formal seats of authority as directors, executives, and partners. A mere several hundred people emerge in each generation as its leaders and spokespersons at the national level. They are almost all between the ages of 50 and 65, and they are usually among the 10 percent to 15 percent of corporate directors who sit on two or more company boards. They also are found more frequently than other executives, bankers, and lawyers on the boards of such nonprofit organizations as foundations, universities, and cultural groups. They are often crucial to the campaign finances of both political parties, and they are more likely than other members of the corporate community to be among the numerous business figures appointed to government positions. Such people are the core of what C. Wright Mills (1956) called the "power elite." More recently, sociologists have called them the "inner group" within the corporate community (Useem, 1978, 1979, 1980).

For all the diversity and complexity of the corporate community and its inner group, the community as a whole is best studied by focusing on the boards of directors of its major corporations. Although all boards are not uniformly important, membership on a board symbolizes a person's importance within the larger corporate community (whether as a member of top management, where day-to-day decision-making power lies in most corporations or as a highly valued financial, legal, or technical adviser who may be in daily, informal contact with the chief executive officer, or even as a person whose visibility adds luster or respectability to the public image of the corporation). That is why we will focus on boards of directors as we turn to the question of the participation of Jews within the corporate elite.

First, however, it would be helpful for us to explore the religious makeup of the American population, and then of the corporate elite. Demographic data indicate that there are about 14 million Jews in the world. The largest number of them is not in Israel, which has only 3 million Jewish citizens, but in the United States, where they number approximately 6 million. And it is the New York metropolitan area, with about 2.4 million, and Los Angeles, with 500,000 (not Tel Aviv or Jerusalem) that have the largest Jewish communities in the world. But as significant as American Jews are within the Jewish population of the world, they make up only 3 percent of the American population; their percentage is declining each year due to small family size compared to other religious-cultural groups and to influxes of non-Jewish immigrants from Mexico, Cuba, Vietnam, and other Third-World countries during the 1970s that far outnumbered the entire Jewish population of the country.

At first glance, it might seem appropriate to use the 3 percent figure as the basis for deciding the degree of underrepresentation or overrepresentation of Jews in the corporate elite. However, since entrance into the corporate community is almost completely predicated upon attainment of a college degree, it might be argued that the comparison should be with all those who attain this educational level. Approximately 8 percent of those who receive college degrees are Jewish. Let us keep these two figures (3 percent of the population, and 8 percent of the college graduates) in mind as we turn to a consideration of the religious backgrounds of the members of the corporate elite.

THE FREQUENCY OF JEWS IN THE CORPORATE ELITE

In 1902, George F. Baer, president of a large company locked in a struggle with trade unionists, wrote in a moment of annoyance with the striking workers that "The rights and interests of the laboring man will be protected and cared for—not by the labor agitators, but by the Christian men to whom God in His infinite wisdom has given the control of property interests in this country" (Rayback, 1966: 211).

Several years later, Baer relaxed a bit in his attitude toward unions, but the inadvertent religious analysis of the corporate community contained in his outburst remains as accurate today as it was for that era. Studies of corporate leaders over the years not only have revealed that control has been for the most part in "Christian" hands, but that from 85 to 90 percent of the leaders have been a very specific kind of Christian from among the many possible—white, male, Anglo-Saxon, and Protestant.

In a study of 190 business leaders between 1901 and 1910 (mostly presidents and chairmen of the largest industrial and financial institutions of the day), William Miller of the Harvard University Research Center in Entrepreneurial History found that 90 percent were Protestant, 7 percent were Catholic, and 3 percent were Jewish (Gregory and Neu, 1952: 200). Mabel Newcomer (1955) found that in 1950, 85 percent of her sample of corporate presidents and chairmen were Protestant, 8.3 percent were Catholic, and 4.6 percent were Jewish. Especially visible in her study were the Episcopalians and Presbyterians, who comprised a little more than 53 percent of the business leaders in her sample even though they comprised only 6.5 percent of the total population. More recently, Frederick Sturdivant and Roy Adler (1976), writing in the *Harvard Business Review*, reported on their study of 444 top executives (again mostly presidents and chairmen) of major American companies in 1975. They found that over 85 percent of the executives were Protestant, and that about 5 percent were Jewish. They concluded that the corporate elite is becoming more homogeneous as time goes by:

> The rather surprising result of all this digging through library materials and comparing of data is that the executives of 1975 form a *more* homogeneous group than those from earlier time periods. Indeed, a more uniform profile is reflected than the one of the supposedly "conforming 1950's." In addition to being exclusively male and Caucasian, predominantly Protestant, Republican, and of eastern U.S. origin, from relatively affluent families, and educated at one of a handful of select universities, as had been the case in the past, the executives in our sample share some new characteristics. Most significantly, the executives are closer together in age, and more of them have little or no work experience outside their companies (Sturdivant and Adler, 1976: 129).

It should be noted that the findings of Newcomer, and of Sturdivant and Adler, are based on the individuals in the samples who indicated their religious affiliations in their *Who's Who in America* biographies. In Newcomer's study, based on the 1950 issue of *Who's Who*, only 44 percent of her sample indicated their religious affiliation. In Sturdivant and Adler's study, based on the 1975 *Who's Who*, only 18 percent gave this information. The inclinations among the corporate elite to include religious preferences in their public images appears to be a declining one, and it is a declining one that could produce a somewhat distorted picture if the tendency is even greater among the Jews.

Our own studies, which approach the problem from a slightly different angle by tracing the corporate connections of publicly identified Jews, suggest that the frequency of Jews within the corporate elite did not change appreciably from the late 1960s to the late 1970s. We looked at the directorships on *Fortune*-level boards held by the members of three groups of Jews over this period.

The first was the governing board of the American Jewish Committee (AJC), the most prestigious Jewish organization at the national level concerned with social and religious issues. The second was the Harmonie Club, the most socially exclusive Jewish men's club in the city of New York. And the third was the Standard Club, Chicago's counterpart to the Harmonie Club. As can be seen in Table 2.1, the very small number of AJC board members on *Fortune*-level boards did not change over that period. Similarly, although there were more directorships held by members of the Harmonie Club and the Standard Club than by the AJC governors, there was no appreciable increase in the number over the period investigated.

TABLE 2.1.
Directorships Held on *Fortune*-Level Boards by Members
of the American Jewish Committee Governing Board,
Harmonie Club, and Standard Club

	1967	1969	1972	1976	1977	1978	1979	1981
American Jewish Committee Governing Board	12	—	—	15	—	12	—	13
Harmonie Club	—	41	—	—	49	—	41	—
Standard Club	—	47	48	—	42	—	—	—

The research we have summarized in this section indicates that Jews have been part of the corporate elite throughout the century, and the frequency of their representation has remained rather constant. The question still remains as to whether they are underrepresented to such an extent that anti-Semitic discrimination may be inferred.

Using either the 3 percent figure (Jews in America) or the 8 percent figure (Jewish college graduates), we conclude that Jews are present in the corporate elite in sufficient numbers that there is no evidence of gross anti-Semitism in the frequency of their involvement. If there have been practices of exclusion, they will have to be found in more subtle analyses than frequency.

ON THE FRINGES: THE LOCATION OF JEWS IN THE CORPORATE ELITE

There is reason to believe that Jews in the corporate elite, although present in representative numbers, are excluded from some business sectors. There is also reason to believe that they are not part of the most economically powerful of corporate entities.

Newcomer found that the Jewish executives were concentrated in the merchandising, entertainment, and mass communication sectors. "Very few are found in heavy industry or public utilities, and none at all among the railroad executives," she pointed out (1955: 46). In addition, she reported that "forty percent of the Jewish group organized their own enterprises" (1955: 48).

A somewhat more impressionistic but wider ranging account by the staff of *Fortune* in 1936 found that Jews were almost totally absent from commercial banking, insurance (except at the agency level in New York), public utilities, and manufacturing, and, contrary to popular belief at the time, they were a small minority in investment banking and communications. (Among organizations in communications, they formed a tiny minority in newspapers and radio, but they were virtually absent from magazines, book publishing, and advertising.) Even in the area of retailing, where Jewish businessmen were thought to predominate because of their visible involvement in department stores and in apparel-store chains, they were, in fact, a minority because of their small presence in five-and-dime, grocery, and drugstore chains. Their only areas of strong involvement were on the fringes of the corporate economy—in clothing, in tobacco buying, in distilling and in scrap iron (*Fortune*, 1936: 132–134).

Periodic surveys by the American Jewish Committee's Institute of Human Relations also indicate that Jews have been very much absent from certain sectors of the corporate elite. In a study of the country's 50 largest commercial banks, for example, the Institute found that only 1.3 percent of the senior officers, and 0.9 percent of the junior executives were Jewish. Forty-five of the 50 banks had no Jews among their senior executives, and 38 of the 50 had none at the lower level. Among nine top banks in New York City, where about half the college graduates are Jewish, the AJC study reported only one Jew among 173 senior-level officers (Kiester, 1972: 10–11).

The situation in newspaper publishing today is very similar to what *Fortune* found to be the case 40 years earlier: "Of the 1748 daily newspapers in the U. S. in 1972, only 3.1 percent were owned by Jews, and the New-house chain, which accounts for half their circulation, avoids the appointment of Jewish editors and publishers" (Karnow, 1974: 13). Our study of the backgrounds of nearly 300 directors in the 25 largest newspaper chains, based upon information developed to study corporate and civic interlocks in major newspapers by sociologist Peter Dreier (Dreier and Weinberg, 1979; Dreier, 1981), found 17 Jewish directors at nine of the companies. The only boards that we could identify with more than two people of Jewish cultural heritage are *The New York Times*, where four descendants of the founding family are among the five Jewish directors, and *The Washington Post*, where three descendants of the publisher who built the newspaper to national stature are on the board. Therefore, although a recent study (Lichter and Rothman, 1982: 43) has shown that a disproportionately high percentage of the best known newspaper journalists and television broadcasters are Jewish, this is not the case in the more important positions of ownership and control.

We also studied (Zweigenhaft, 1982) the location of Jews in the corporate elite by systematically looking at the trustees of charitable foundations in the mid-1970s; our study was made possible by the first appearance of a biographical volume, *Trustees of Wealth* (1975), which lists all those people who were directors of any of several thousand foundations. Because of the particularly important role philanthropy has played in the Jewish community, we reasoned that the boards of charitable foundations might be a good place to look for those Jews most likely to be prominent members of the corporate elite. As Naomi Cohen (1972: 47), author of an insightful history of the American Jewish Committee, writes in explaining the reason why such organizations as the AJC are able to attract the donations of respected Jewish leaders:

> Philanthropists gained the admiration of Jews and non-Jews, and certainly a position of leadership within the Jewish community. Since Jews were generally barred from posts of command in old established civic causes—charity organizations, museums, private libraries—that were the purview of the American elite, they could satisfy their ambitions in Jewish areas. And, because of the weakened position of the syna-

gogue, the philanthropic maze became increasingly the locus of Jewish communal power.

For this study, we first selected those people who, by nature of the club, civic, or religious affiliations they listed in their biographies, could be assumed to be Jewish. A total of 219 people was selected in this manner. An equal number of non-Jewish people listed in *Trustees of Wealth* was randomly selected. The selection process was a sample matched by residence such that the number of names chosen from each state corresponded to the number in the Jewish sample. For example, since there were 28 Jewish trustees from California, 28 non-Jewish trustees were selected from that state. In addition, in almost every case, we matched the residences of the non-Jewish group with those of the Jewish sample in terms of city as well as state.

When we checked the two groups in *Who's Who in America*, 1975–76, for their presence or absence in the corporate elite, we found there were more Jewish than non-Jewish foundation trustees on *Fortune*-level boards: 75 of the 219 Jewish trustees sat on one or more boards, but only 54 of the 219 non-Jewish trustees did so. However, the Jewish directors were less likely to be on the boards of the largest corporations. Although they were on the boards of 13 of the top 100 industrials, the gentiles were on 22 such boards. When we focused on the ten largest industrials, we found only one Jewish director in the sample, but there were four non-Jewish directors. Or, to consider the pattern of representation from another perspective, 59 percent of the boards with gentile directors were among the top 200 industrials, as compared with only 33 percent of the boards with Jewish directors.*

There also were differences in representation on the boards of the top 50 in banks, diversified financials, life insurance, and retailing. Among the 150 companies in the three financial sectors, there were 22 gentile directors and 13 Jewish directors. On the other hand, there were 11 Jews and only 3 non-Jews among the top 50 retails. Public utility and transportation companies showed no differences.*

We traced the new corporate directorships added by the people in these two samples through the next three editions of *Who's Who in America* to 1981 and found no changes in this general pattern. Twelve of the Jewish trustees reported 15 new directorships and the same number of gentiles added 17 to their biographies, but once again the non-Jews were more likely to join the largest corporations. For example, seven of the ten industrial boards added by the gentiles were in the top 200, but only three of the 13 added by the Jews were at that level.*

---

*See Appendix 1 for a version of this paragraph that includes tests of statistical significance.

Our systematic findings are in accord with the impressions of the Jewish members of the corporate elite whom we interviewed in New York, Boston, Chicago, Los Angeles, and other large cities. Jay Pritzker of Chicago, a member of one of the richest families in America and reportedly worth from $700 million to $1 billion, obviously has not been hampered by any anti-Semitism there may be within the business community. However, when asked about directorships held by successful Jewish businessmen, he said that he doubted that there are more Jews on boards than in the recent past. "I don't see many Jews on gentile boards, and my guess is there are no more Jews on boards in general than there were ten or twenty years ago, at least not in Chicago." Simon Rifkind, a corporate lawyer in New York since the 1920s who sat on the boards of Loews and Revlon before he retired, also did not see any change:

> The best place to look if you want to is in the banking fraternity. Jews have traditionally been successful bankers, and yet if you look at most of the commercial banks you will not find a Jewish name at all, maybe a rarity here and there of late, but almost none. The same is true of the major insurance companies. I would say the same is true of most of the bigger corporations. I have not made a check to see how many Jews are on the Fortune 500, but I'm very sure that you will find the Jews are members of boards of firms that have made the 500 which are of Jewish origin or Jewish dominated—not many of the other kind.

Nor did Sidney Brody of Los Angeles, head of his family investment company and a director of the largest bank in the city, think that things had changed on the West Coast. "Not to any great extent," he replied to our question.

Our findings, then, while showing that Jews are part of the corporate elite, give no support to the claim by General Brown that Jews are in control of banking and newspapers, let alone any other part of the economy. We now turn to the question of how Jews become part of the corporate elite to see if their pathways to the top are similar to those of other directors.

PATHWAYS TO THE TOP

Founders

Jews in the corporate elite most often are directors on the boards of companies that were founded or purchased by Jewish individuals or families. For example, of the 116 directorships held by the 75 Jewish directors in our study of 219 foundation trustees, we estimate that about one-third of the positions were in such companies. Thus, for example, five were on the board of Food Fair; three were on the boards of Inland Steel and Loews; and two were on each of the boards of CBS, Cerro, Crown-Zellerbach, Cone Mills, General Dynamics, Giant Foods, MCA, Sears, Seagrams, and Stop and Shop. The histories and boards of Witco Chemical, Levi Strauss, and General Dynamics are typical of corporations in this group.

In 1896, Eli Wishnick, referred to by his grandson as "a Talmudic scholar, a part-time rabbi, a horse trader and a part-time merchant" (Wishnick, 1976: 10), came to America from Russia with his oldest son. He made his way to Chicago where he was able to set up a small store. He then saved enough money to send for his wife and seven other children. The youngest son, Robert, won a scholarship to the Armour Institute of Technology, where he studied chemical engineering. After receiving his degree, he took a job as a chemist with the American Magnesium Products Company and studied law at night. In 1920, with two friends, he started the Wishnick-Tumpeer Chemical Company.

The company expanded its operations over the years, changed its name in 1944 to Witco, and went public in 1958. William Wishnick, Robert's son, who became chairman of the board in 1964, explains how representatives of the two financial advising groups each were elected to "chairs" on the Board:

> Since the early 50s, various people had been knocking on our door wanting to discuss making us public. One of the most diligent of these was Harcourt Amory of Smith Barney & Co., so when the Witco Board decided to go public, they chose Smith Barney because of their expertise in chemical company financing. At the same time, they chose Goldman, Sachs, which did not represent any major chemical company but was active in acquisitions, some of which we felt might be brought to us. Gus Levy of Goldman, Sachs and Harcourt Amory of Smith Barney were asked to join our Board and both of them were of great help in helping our company make its progress after going public. Gus Levy, of course, is still with us as a Director, and the Smith Barney chair is now occupied by Bill Grant (Wishnick, 1976: 26).

As of 1981, Witco was the 227th largest industrial corporation on *Fortune*'s list, and there were 15 members on its board. Seven of the men on the board were full-time employees of the company ("inside directors"). Among the eight "outside directors," William R. Grant was still on the board, but no longer with Smith Barney; Bruce F. Wesson sat in the Smith Barney chair, and another partner from Goldman, Sachs had replaced Gus Levy when he died in 1979. Also on the board was a senior partner from Bachner, Talley & Mantell, which provides Witco with legal advice when it is needed. And there is a nonemployee member of the founding family, John H. Wishnick, on the board, along with business friends of top management.

On all these dimensions—the proportion of inside and outside directors, the inclusion of financial and legal advisers, the presence of family representatives and business colleagues—the board of Witco Chemical does not differ from those of most other corporations. Only the Jewish heritage of the majority of its members makes this board different from many others.

In 1844, Levi Strauss came to America. Like so many of the German Jews whose children were to become known in New York City around the turn of the century as "our crowd," he came from Bavaria. And like many Jewish lads at the time who were considered men at the age of 13, he left, alone, for America at the age of 14. Six years after his arrival in New York, Levi Strauss sailed around Cape Horn to California. As one writer put it, "He did not come to be a gold miner—hoping to survive in the desert heat and mountain cold on sow belly, sourdough, jack rabbits or, as a last resort, by eating his own burro. Strauss came to sell merchandise" (Harris, 1979: 237). After spending a few months selling merchandise out of a tiny store in Sacramento, Strauss had saved enough money to move to San Franscisco. There, in a store on California St., he sold "everything from corsets and petticoats to umbrellas."

Legend has it that in response to complaints from miners that their pockets, which were frequently crammed with mining tools and rock samples, wore off too fast, one of Strauss' tailors had a local harness-maker rivet the pocket corners with copper. It worked so well that in 1873 Strauss and the tailor took out a 17-year patent on the use of copper rivets to strengthen work clothes. They were able to renew the patent in 1890, and by the time the renewal ran out, the reputation of Levi's was well established.

Levi Strauss died a bachelor in 1902. His heirs, the Sterns, Koshlands, and Haases, have remained active in the corporation. When Levi Strauss went public in 1971, *The New York Times* reported that "the offering created at least 28 instant millionaires" (Harris, 1979: 255).

In 1981, Levi Strauss was ranked as the 138th largest industrial on *Fortune's* list. Its 21-member board includes six Jews—three members of the Haas family, two nonfamily executives who have risen in the company, and the chairman of another Jewish-founded company. The Levi Strauss board is fairly typical of Jewish-founded companies—there is a tendency for them to end up with a majority of non-Jews.

Arie Crown left Latvia in the early 1860s at the age of 14. He arrived in New York City and made his way to St. Louis. From St. Louis, he went to Chicago in response to an advertisement for a salesman. The job, however, was selling bibles, and it didn't quite work out. Crown stayed in Chicago and became a small manufacturer of suspenders. A fire in 1898 destroyed his shop, and Arie, his wife, and their seven children struggled along barely making ends meet. In 1921, two of Arie's sons were able to borrow the $10,000 needed to start Material Service Corporation, a building supply company. Though there were about 80 building supply companies in Chicago at that time, Material Service, under the leadership of Arie's sons Henry and Irving, began to outstrip the competition. One reason they were able to do so was their discovery that it was much cheaper to bring building supplies to Chicago by boat rather than by rail. By 1959, when Material Services merged with the larger General Dynamics in what amounted to a friendly corporate takeover, it was the largest building supply firm in the world and had a net worth of $72 million..

As a result of the merger with General Dynamics, the Crowns received $125 million worth of General Dynamics stock, and Henry Crown became a member of the board. However, he ended up in conflict with Roger Lewis, the man he had picked to run the company. In a complicated set of maneuvers, Lewis and his sympathizers on the board exercised their right, by terms of the earlier merger deal, to ask Crown either to sell his preferred stock or to convert it to common stock. This left Crown with two unpleasant alternatives. If he opted for conversion to common stock, he would lose about $24 million but retain his position of influence. If he sold the preferred stock back to the company, he would receive some $104 million, but he would lose control of General Dynamics and have to pay capital gains taxes as well.

Most observers thought Crown would convert to common stock, but instead he took the $104 million and left, or so it seemed. In fact, he had sold at the equivalent of $48 a share after taxes at a time when the common stock was selling for only $39 a share and he began to buy common stock bit by bit on the market with the money he had received. Late in 1969, three years after he had left the board, Crown joined with a close friend (also worth hundreds of millions) in a serious effort to regain control of the company. As his holdings rose from 4 percent to 11 percent of the stock (a very high percentage in a major corporation), Crown periodically would call Lewis, his old nemesis, to let him know what was going on. In our interview with him, Crown depicted the subsequent events in the following way:

> I called up the chairman of the company, and told him—every time we bought stock in the company, I'd send word to him again so we were doing nothing that wasn't right on the table—and so he knew when we had 4 percent, 6 percent, 8 percent. Now I told him we had 11 percent.

Well, I think this took him by surprise. This was on a Wednesday or a Thursday, I remember. Saturday morning, the President of our coal company called me up at home and said "Roger Lewis just called me, and he asked for your phone number at home."

Sure enough, Roger called me and said, "Are you going to be in Chicago next Monday and Tuesday?" I said yes. He came in and said, "What have you got in mind?" I laughed, and said, "I knew that question was coming. I haven't a damn thing in mind." The President of the coal company told me that same day when he drove him back to the airport, "He was very disappointed when he left your office. He said you wouldn't tell him anything." He just wasn't believing we didn't have anything in mind.

Well, actually, six months after that he called me and asked me if I would meet with the company attorney and bring one of our people along. I did that, met him at the Waldorf. He kept pleading with me and our attorney that I go back on the board with him. I said, "Why should I go back on the board?" And he said, "Well, you've got an interest now, you didn't have it before."

Anyway, he finally offered us six directors out of 14 (he'd still have eight). We did that for one year, agreeing to his having eight. And the understanding was that he and I were going to pick a President. He was to be the Chairman and, of course, I was to be the Chairman of the Executive Committee, as I was before.

Crown and Lewis were unable to agree on a president, and Crown was convinced in any case that the company was being "terribly managed." By the end of the year, Lewis was out (taking his management skills to Washington, where he became the head of Amtrak), and Crown was back in control of General Dynamics. The net worth of the company rose from $200 million when Crown took it over again to almost $1 billion in 1980, at which time it was 83rd on *Fortune*'s list. In addition, as of 1980, 5 of the 16 General Dynamics directors were Jewish, including Henry's son Lester, who also sits as an outside director (and the only Jewish director) on the boards of TWA and Esmark. In 1975, *Business Week* wrote that "Henry Crown is patriarch of one of the largest constellations of wealth in the U. S." Lester was referred to as "patriarch-in-waiting."

Not all companies founded or subsequently controlled by Jews have provided continuing opportunities to other Jewish businessmen. Sears, Roebuck—a company that was founded by a gentile, Richard Sears, but which became a dominant economic force under the dual ownership of Sears and his Jewish partner, Julius Rosenwald—provides perhaps the most striking example. After Sears died in 1909, the Rosenwald family became the principal owners. Yet from 1939 to 1954, the Chairman of the Board, Robert Elkington Wood, did not allow Jews to be hired as buyers or for any executive positions within the company. Lessing Rosenwald,

Julius' son, who followed Julius as Chairman of the Board and preceded Wood, had this to say about Wood's anti-Semitism: "It was obvious. During Wood's administration every Jew in an important position was relieved and not one was hired." Yet neither Lessing Rosenwald nor his brothers and sisters, the dominant Sears stockholders, said anything to Wood, because, according to Rosenwald: "He was powerful and popular and was doing a superb job of running the company for the stockholders in terms of profits and dominance" (Harris, 1979: 320–321).

Even today, some of the corporations founded by Jews would prefer to reduce the number of Jewish directors on their boards. As one of the men we interviewed said of his board:

> It's about half Jewish. I'm making every effort to change it as rapidly as I can away from being a Jewish company. It just happened that way. You know we were a small company and went public and the board members were friends of my father's. That's the normal thing. Over the years we got more and more outside directorships. But when we look at new directors now, it's a negative thing if you're Jewish. I'm not saying we don't do it, but it's a negative thing, it's more of a plus to be non-Jewish. I think it's bad for our company to have any image as a Jewish company.

Some Jewish-founded companies have ended up with few or no Jewish directors without any explicit effort to do so. "It's not a case of discrimination," said Joseph L. Block, the retired president of Inland Steel, a company founded by his Jewish forebearers at the turn of the century and one that had three Jewish directors throughout most of the 1970s. "It's just the way the chips have fallen. The last president before the present president was Jewish. It just so happens that right now there isn't a Jewish director. Next year there might be."

Members of founding families not only sit on their own boards, and sometimes provide seats on these boards for other Jews, but they are among the Jews most likely to be invited to join prominent gentile boards. No better example exists than the Lazarus brothers, Ralph and Maurice, executives and directors of Federated Department Stores; their company ranked 10th among retails in 1981 and now encompasses several of the most famous of the German-Jewish department stores in large cities across the country. Ralph Lazarus, the chairman of Federated, also sits on the boards of Chase Manhattan Bank, General Electric, and Scott Paper. Maurice Lazarus, chairman of the finance committee of Federated (after many years as an executive in its Boston store, Filene's) is on the board of Massachusetts Mutual, Itek, and New England Telephone.

In the case of Maurice Lazarus, it was a combination of business experience and friendship that led to these directorships. "It's the custom for the phone company to have at least one person from retailing because of knowledge of marketing and demographics," he explained. As for Massachusetts Mutual, the chairman of its board happened to be on the board of New England Telephone, liked what he saw of Maurice Lazarus on that board, and asked him to join the insurance company board as well.

But not all Jews on boards are founders or descendants of founders. There are other pathways to the top as well.

The Investment Banker

In the 1920s, in response to the continued publication of viciously anti-Semitic articles in Henry Ford's Dearborn *Independent*, many Jews, and apparently even some non-Jews, refused to buy Ford automobiles. According to Stanley Feldstein (1978: 225): "The Jewish press reminded its readers that the 'next time you ride in a Ford car, think of what Ford said about you,' and the American Jewish Committee urged Jewish newspapers not to publish advertisements of Ford merchandise." And yet, in 1956, Ford Motor made headlines by asking Sidney J. Weinberg, a Jew, to be on its board. How did this turn of events come about?

Sidney Weinberg was a partner in Goldman, Sachs, one of the most eminent investment banking firms on Wall Street, and certainly one of the most prominent among a small group of German-Jewish firms that once worked closely with each other and played a major role in financing the development of large retail firms. Weinberg, the son of a Brooklyn wine merchant who himself became a partner on Wall Street with the small firm of Filer & Company in 1919, joined Goldman, Sachs in 1907 as an office boy, at a time when all the partners were still Goldman and Sachs relatives.

In 1927, 20 years after he came to work for the firm, Weinberg was taken in as a partner. By then the firm had changed completely in character. The influence of the most powerful Goldman had ended abruptly due to his strong pro-German attitudes during the war, and there were no Sachs heirs who took an active role. Indeed, the top partner in the firm at the time Sidney gained his new status was Waddill Catchings, a Southerner of non-Jewish background. Within a few years, Weinberg was the senior partner in the firm and a director of several companies. He was becoming part of the inner group within the corporate community.

And, as is not atypical for members of the inner group, Weinberg became involved in policy-discussion organizations where business leaders meet to discuss the major issues of the day, sometimes with the help of academic experts and government officials. In particular, he became a member of the Business Advisory Council, a group formed in the early 1930s by the Secretary of Commerce to provide government leaders, including the President, with business advice (McQuaid, 1979). Weinberg also served as assistant treasurer of the Democratic Party in 1932 and 1936, bringing him into contact with the major donors on that side of the political fence.

It was at a meeting of the Business Advisory Council in 1947 that Sidney Weinberg first met Henry Ford II, the young heir to his grandfather's company who had been installed as its chairman in the mid-1940s after his father died unexpectedly. They became friends at the off-the-record weekend meetings the 60 Council members hold four times a year with government officials. As Weinberg later said, "The Business Advisory Council is a great place to get to know people."

So it was that in the fall of 1953, when the Ford Foundation was preparing to offer a big chunk of its stock to the public, Henry Ford II employed Sidney Weinberg to handle the family's affairs. Weinberg spent half his working time for two years on this project. The major problem was to come up with a plan, agreeable to all involved parties, that would pay the Ford family for transferring its voting rights in the company to public shares that would be sold by the foundation. Although the Ford Foundation owned 88 percent of all Ford shares, all were of the nonvoting variety, as were an additional 2 percent owned by Ford directors, officers, and employees. The remaining 10 percent were in the hands of the Ford family. These were the shares with voting power, thus giving complete control of the company to the family, and therein lay the problem. In order to be accepted by the New York Stock Exchange, the Ford Foundation's stock would have to have voting power, which required some agreement between the family and the trustees of the foundation. In his 1956 *New Yorker* profile of Weinberg, E. J. Kahn, Jr., outlined Weinberg's task as follows:

> As Weinberg set about his assignment, he could see that any plan he devised would have to be acceptable to the Ford family, to the Foundation's trustees, to the New York Stock Exchange, and to the Internal Revenue Service. The last party was a far from inconsiderable one, since if it should rule that whatever benefits the Ford family got out of the deal weren't tax-free, the Fords wouldn't be interested, and if the Foundation's tax-exempt status should be questioned, it wouldn't be interested. Weinberg prepared some fifty-odd reorganization plans: under the one that was finally approved by all parties, the Ford family increased its equity in the company by 1.74 percent—which, reckoned in terms of the stock's value on the day it was marketed, amounted to a paper gain of nearly sixty million dollars.

After this deft financial work for the Ford family, Weinberg was asked to be an outside director for Ford Motor Company. Although his passage from financial advisor to director was spectacular and widely publicized because it took place at Ford Motor Company (founded by a man well known for his virulent anti-Semitism), it was an example of a time-honored manner of becoming an outside director. In fact, Myles Mace (1971: 128) devotes an entire chapter of his book on boards of directors to "Investment Bankers as Directors," and starts it by saying that "One of the principal sources of outside directors for large and medium-sized companies is the investment banking firm and its partners."

One other Jew joined the Ford board during the years Weinberg was a member, and Weinberg probably played a role in his selection. In 1965, Joseph Frederick Cullman 3rd, the chairman of the board and chief executive officer of Philip Morris, was asked to join the board of Ford Motor Company. Cullman knew Henry Ford II "pretty well" because Ford had gone to Hotchkiss, as had Cullman, and had been a classmate of Cullman's younger brother, Edgar. Cullman also had gone on an Eastern European trip with Ford, sponsored by *Time* magazine. But as Cullman thinks back on his selection to the Ford board, he attributes it primarily to Sidney Weinberg, for Weinberg played, he told us, "a critical role in the development of the outside directors." Though he could not say "categorically" that Weinberg got him on, he did say: "I'm sure that if Sidney Weinberg hadn't wanted me I wouldn't have gone on the board, and I rather suspect that he gave me a little nudge."

Sidney Weinberg died in 1969, but his place at Goldman, Sachs, and on many corporate boards, has been taken over by one of his sons, John Weinberg. When we asked him why he was on the BF Goodrich board, he replied, "I took my father's place on that board. I took his place at Kraft also." Later in the interview, he indicated that the same thing had happened at Cluett-Peabody: "That was one of the early companies that Goldman, Sachs financed; my father was on that board, then I went on the board." At Witco Chemical, discussed earlier in the chapter, he was the partner who replaced Gustave Levy when he died.

One of John Weinberg's board memberships, Knight-Ridder (a newspaper chain) demonstrates the typical way in which an investment banker ends up on a board: "Oh, that's a company I worked on and we went public [handled the issuance of public stock] for the Knight newspapers." The other board he is on, Seagrams, is owned by a wealthy Jewish family, the Bronfmans, who have members in both Canada and the United States. His presence on this board illustrates the mixture of friendship and business that characterizes many invitations to join boards: "Edgar Bronfman's one of my closest friends in the world, and he asked me to go on his board; we'd done a lot of work for them."

From John Weinberg's point of view, the question of Jewishness is not an important one to any of these companies: "In the early days there probably was a lot of anti-Semitism. Today it's just a question of who works there, and who gets ahead and who does things. Now it's really professionalism."

Weinberg also noted that his own firm is integrated religiously, a development that is not at all uncommon for the several investment banking firms that were founded by Jews in the heyday of the investment banker: "At Goldman, Sachs, for example, I'm co-chairman of this firm and my co-chairman is not Jewish. We're mixed completely. We have Jews here, we have non-Jews. The same thing at Lehmans or the other old Jewish firms."

The Lehmans to which John Weinberg was referring is Lehman Brothers Kuhn Loeb, perhaps the best known in recent years of the investment houses founded by a Jewish family. Founded in 1850, and admitting partners only with the name Lehman for its first 75 years, it was the oldest investment banking partnership in existence when it became a public corporation in 1975. Beginning as a buyer and seller of commodities, particularly cotton, it did not become seriously involved in investment banking until Philip Lehman joined with his good friend Henry Goldman at Goldman, Sachs to underwrite 14 major securities offerings between 1906 and 1914 (Wise, 1957).

As potent as the working relationship between Lehman Brothers and Goldman, Sachs was for a few years, it was not destined to last. As the next generation of partners took over in the respective firms, there was a gradual falling out, and in 1925, a formal agreement was signed that specified which of the two firms would have primary responsibility for each of the corporations they had financed jointly. And like Goldman, Sachs, Lehman Brothers gradually took in non-Jewish partners as the two firms went their separate ways (Wise, 1957; see, also, Wise, 1963 and 1968).

From the late 1920s through the 1960s when Sidney Weinberg reigned at Goldman, Sachs, the top partner at Lehman Brothers, Robert Lehman, was more than his match in power and status, sitting on several corporate boards, amassing an art collection worth over $50 million dollars, and raising funds for the Republican Party. When Robert Lehman died, his place was taken by Frederick L. Erhman, a San Franciscan of German-Jewish origins, who joined the firm in the early 1940s.

But the Lehman Brothers Kuhn Loeb of today is a very different place. After Robert Lehman's death it became a corporation rather than a private partnership, and in 1975 its 84 corporate partners created a formal management hierarchy and selected a non-Jew, Peter G. Peterson (a former Bell & Howell president and one-time Secretary of Commerce) to head the firm. The new structure was not to the liking of everyone, and four partners, all gentiles, moved to the small and predominantly-Jewish firm of Lazard, Frères, whose most visible partner in the 1970s was a wealthy Jewish immigrant from Poland and Austria, Felix Rohatyn, the engineer of several big mergers for Lazard customers and the fiscal taskmaster of New York City during its budget crisis of the mid-1970s.

In 1977, Lehman Brothers provided Wall Street with another surprise when it absorbed the venerable German-Jewish investment firm, Kuhn, Loeb. At one time Kuhn, Loeb's partners had included such famous names in the annals of American finance as Jacob Schiff, financier of dozens of railroads and second only to J. P. Morgan as the Wall Street kingpin during the era of great mergers; Felix Warburg, one of the architects of the Federal Reserve Bank; and, not least, John M. Schiff, who married into a gentile banking family and served through the 1970s as a director of such well-known firms as Getty Oil, Uniroyal, Kennecott Copper, Westinghouse, CIT Financial, and A&P. The changed role of investment banking in an era of institutional investors spelled the end for this private partnership.

Our interview with a former Lehman Brothers partner, F. Warren Hellman, provided further insight into the ways in which investment bankers end up on boards. Born into German-Jewish wealth in California in 1934, and related to the Haas and Koshland families of Levi Strauss, he joined Lehman Brothers in 1959 and became a partner in 1962. He left Lehman Brothers in 1975 to start a small three-person investment firm in Boston—Hellman, Gal Investment Associates—with another former Lehman partner and a security analyst from Loeb Rhoades & Co. (yet another Jewish-founded firm that found a merger partner when its leader for the past several decades, John L. Loeb, retired). However, Hellman retains his ties with his old friends through a directorship on Lehman Corporation, a large investment fund managed by Lehman Brothers Kuhn Loeb.

Hellman tries to hold a limit on the number of boards he belongs to at any given time. As he put it, "I don't really like to be a director very much. I either really like to be involved very deeply, such as at Twentieth Century Fox where I'm on the executive committee, I talk to the management daily, and I'm an integral part of the direction of the company, or I'd rather not do it at all."

In addition to Twentieth Century Fox (Fortune's #337 in 1981), Hellman sits on the boards of Gulton (#897) and Peabody (#392). He first joined the board at Gulton in the early 1960s when it was "a much

smaller company" because Gulton "was a Lehman client." His involvement in Peabody began late in the 1960s when he and a group of
friends bought controlling interest in the company, brought in new
management, and built the company up in what was "a venture capital
deal." But, unlike his considerable involvement as a director at Twentieth
Century Fox, Hellman described his Peabody directorship as one in which
he has decreasing personal involvement:

> Peabody has kind of slid away from me. I don't know many of the people
> in the company. I go to directors' meetings and I sit there and I'm kind of
> a stiff—they say this division earned $200,000 last month as opposed
> to $100,000 the month before and my eyes kind of glaze over. I guess
> I would prefer to be on boards where we have investments, where I
> have my money on the line, or of companies where I like the manage-
> ment very much, and they feel they really need my services and I'm
> interested in the business.

Though Hellman indicated that he is aware of anti-Semitic discrimination in the corporate world, his view is that it is less of a problem
for investment bankers than for others:

> From the standpoint of the company, investment bankers tend to make
> fairly decent directors. They have a fairly broad outlook on things,
> and fairly broad experiences. I think that's an area where being Jewish
> or not being Jewish doesn't mean very much.

Investment banking, then, has contributed numerous Jewish directors to the corporate elite, some of them as famous and powerful in
their own right as the corporate founders. The partnerships that these
men or their families created at one time formed a significant community
of influence on Wall Street, rivaling the "Yankee" firms which were
founded in the same era by men who had made their way to New York
from New England.

However, these once-tight partnerships have evolved along with
the rest of Wall Street, and it is doubtful that any of them will be
perceived as particularly Jewish in the future. And only a few of the
investment banking firms—e.g., Merrill, Lynch; First Boston; Morgan,
Stanley; Goldman, Sachs; and Lehman Brothers Kuhn Loeb—will remain
powers to be reckoned with in financial circles. Others, and most notably
Lazard, Frères, will retain some significance in the area of mergers, but
the day of a large and powerful investment banking fraternity seems to
be past, and with its passing a major avenue of advancement for many
Jewish directors has been lost.

The Corporate Lawyer

Rare is the American lawyer who has dozens of partners as well as even more associates who help the partners with their cases, yet this is the typical situation for the relatively few corporate lawyers who work with large law factories that handle the legal problems of the top banks and corporations, and sometimes their political problems as well.

Traditionally, corporate lawyers have come from a handful of prestigious law schools such as Harvard, Yale, Stanford, and Columbia, and traditionally they have excluded Jews, even though Jews have graduated from many of the major law schools in large numbers. A few Jews served these firms as associates, learning the ropes and doing the routine work, but very few became partners. Most Jewish lawyers went straight to work for smaller Jewish firms, or looked for positions in government.

Simon Rifkind came to America from Russia in 1910, at the age of nine, speaking only Yiddish. While his father worked as "a small time woolen merchant," Rifkind studied English (as well as Hebrew and the Talmud) at a parochial school for East European immigrants. When he finished high school, he attended the City College of New York (CCNY), and then went on to receive his law degree from Columbia. He explained the options open to him when he finished law school in the following way:

> When I came to the bar, in 1925, it was utterly impossible for any Jewish lad to be employed by any of the major non-Jewish law firms. Maybe if you looked with a microscope you might find somebody in an office of some consequence, a mistake somebody had made. It was utterly hopeless for a Jewish boy to even go look for a job at any of those offices, any of what we now regard as the major law offices of the city. And, of course, I had a good record at the law school, I had no door that would open to me in any of those offices. I went to work for a Jewish law firm when I first left law school.

But about a year later, Robert Wagner was elected Senator from New York, and hired Rifkind to be his "legislative secretary" (a position now referred to as legislative assistant). Rifkind worked for Wagner's small law firm in New York as well as for Wagner in Washington ("In those days, the Senate sessions were very brief, they lasted only a couple of months a year, so you could afford to continue your private professional pursuits, as he and I did"), and soon became a partner. He was aware that becoming a partner in a predominantly gentile firm, even a small one, was highly unusual at that time, and essentially a result of his having done so by way of his political appointment: "When I joined Wagner, of course, that was not a Jewish office . . . but that was an unusual thing. It happened as a result of the fact that I was recommended to Senator Wagner by the dean of my law school and that I joined him in one capacity that I then merged into the other capacity."

After fifteen years with the firm, Rifkind left to become a federal judge in 1941. When he left the bench in 1950, he joined the firm that came to be known as Paul, Weiss, Rifkind, Wharton & Garrison; it was one of the first "integrated" and politically liberal firms in New York, and Rifkind played a key role in making it one of the top firms in the city. Among its major clients were Twentieth Century Fox, Field Enterprises, the *New York Post*, Kinney Services, and Revlon, with Rifkind sitting on the boards of the last two. In 1957, the firm opened a Chicago office headed by Adlai Stevenson, but it closed down when all four Chicago partners ended up in the Kennedy Administration (Hoffman, 1973). President Kennedy's main speechwriter and political advisor, Ted Sorenson, joined the firm in the mid-1960s, as did former Secretary of Labor and Supreme Court Justice Arthur Goldberg for a brief period.

As noted earlier in the chapter, Rifkind does not think there have been any changes in the religious makeup of corporate boards. But he believes major changes have occurred in the big law firms:

> Today there is still some impediment to Jewish lads in some offices, but that solid closed wall is no longer there. Today there are lots of openings. The whole business has changed. Today top young law students don't go knocking at doors to look for jobs. The big offices send out teams to recruit them every year, as we do, and the demand for young men and women with brains, talent, capacity, assiduity, and all the stuff that it takes to make a high-powered lawyer, is very much in demand. They're being competed for intensely, the price of their services going up to astronomical levels. So the world has changed in that respect, and there's no longer a closed wall incapable of penetration as it was the first twenty years of my practice.

George Szabad has a very different background from Rifkind, and he graduated from law school 14 years later, but his experiences as a young lawyer were similar. Szabad's parents were wealthy Polish Jews, a very different financial circumstance than that of most Eastern European Jews. Szabad's maternal grandfather owned the largest cigarette factory in Poland before it was nationalized in the 1920s, and his father's family "had interests in several factories."

When Szabad's father died, his mother married Jim Akston, an American who worked for General Motors. General Motors failed in Poland, and, after trying other work for several years, Akston convinced Szabad's mother to come to America in the 1930s. This, as Szabad pointed out to us, was "like a lottery ticket," for he subsequently lost half his family during the Nazi holocaust.

Szabad, like Rifkind, took English lessons when he arrived, then went on to do extremely well at Columbia Law School. Yet, when he graduated in 1939, it was hard to get a job, for "there was clear discrimination against Jews." In fact, he told us that while one of his classmates was being interviewed by a senior partner of a downtown firm, he was asked to point out all the Jews on the *Columbia Law Review* masthead "just so they wouldn't make a mistake and, say, hire a Szabad, who was kind of a peculiar animal, and get stuck with a Jew." He worked for a small Jewish firm in New York, then went to Washington, where he worked as a government lawyer for five years before returning to New York to join a predominantly Jewish law firm now called Blum, Haimoff, Gersen, Lipson, Slavin & Szabad. One of his clients was a Jewish-founded firm, Burndy Corporation, a manufacturer of electrical connectors for a variety of uses. He became its secretary, with the title of vice president, and a member of its board of directors, the only directorship he holds in a *Fortune*-level company.

Although Szabad's legal and business connections have remained more with other Jews than did those of Rifkind, he also sees changes for the better for Jewish lawyers within non-Jewish law firms. "Needless to say," he concludes, "today it's completely different, it's open."

Richard Sherwood, a partner in O'Melveny & Meyers, the largest and most eminent law firm in Los Angeles, thinks that things have changed for Jewish lawyers in Los Angeles as well. According to Sherwood (who is about 10th in seniority among 90 partners but does not sit on any boards because he is primarily involved in litigation) there had not been any Jewish lawyers in the firm from the turn of the century until he was hired in 1955. Now there are 10 or 12 Jewish partners, and a slightly higher proportion of Jews among the 160 associates. This story, he says, has been repeated "with differing paces" at the other large law firms in the city.

Sherwood also notes that Jewish partners he knows in his and other law firms have joined the boards of gentile-founded firms. If Jews continue to be taken into previously gentile law firms, as seems entirely likely, it may be that this avenue to the boardroom will take up any slack left by the gradual decline of investment bankers.

The Academic Expert

Yet another pathway to the corporate elite is that of the academic expert. Those who travel this path typically obtain postgraduate degrees in some academic field and either through research or consulting (or both) come to be known as useful resources to those in the corporate elite. Then, like the lawyers we have just discussed, in the process of providing their skills to those already in the corporate elite, they become part of that elite. We will consider the careers of three academic experts: Alan Greenspan, Arthur Burns, and Daniel Yankelovich.

Alan Greenspan is a man of Jewish background, although a little different in philosophy from most Jews in that he is a great admirer of the superindividualism of Ayn Rand. He has never worked for a corporation. Nor is he an investment banker or a corporate lawyer. And yet in 1977 he joined the boards of Morgan Guaranty Trust, Mobil, and General Foods, three of the larger corporate entities in the world.

Greenspan followed another fairly typical pathway to the top, that of expert advisor. He is an economist and business consultant (a bit of a self-taught economist, his critics claim, but an economist nonetheless, with an M.A. in the subject from New York University in 1950). Following his graduation, Greenspan lost little time in founding his own consulting and forecasting firm, Townsend-Greenspan & Co., of which he was president from 1954 to 1974 before taking his first full-time job with the government in July, 1975 as chairman of President Nixon's (and then President Ford's) Council of Economic Advisers.

Greenspan made a name for himself on Wall Street in the 1960s, but what moved him into the inner circles was his considerable involvement in the Nixon Presidential campaign in 1968. Following Nixon's victory, Greenspan became a consultant to several government agencies, including Treasury, the Federal Reserve Board, and the Council of Economic Advisers, as well as serving as a member of various task forces and commissions. His Nixon ties also brought him more consultantships in the private nongovernmental sectors, as a senior advisor on a Brookings Institution panel on economic activity, and as a member of *Time*'s board of economists. It was during this period that he also joined two boards in the corporate community: Dreyfus Fund, a mutual investment fund, and General Cable. Nonetheless, it was his three years on the Council of Economic Advisers that moved him to the very top; he joined the boards of Morgan, Mobil, and General Foods within months after he left the Council, thereby providing these companies with a "reading" on the economy as well as an insider's observations on how to deal with the federal government.

Only slightly different is the career of another economist of Jewish heritage, Arthur F. Burns, who has served on the board of Mutual Life of New York since the late 1950s with time out for service as chair of the Federal Reserve Board for the first eight years in the 1970s. Burns was born in Austria in 1904 and came to the United States in 1910. He received his Ph.D. in 1934 from Columbia University and stayed there as a professor while at the same time serving as a researcher for the National Bureau for Economic Research (NBER), one of several think tanks financed by the corporate community that focuses almost exclusively on economic policies. From 1945 to 1953, he served as NBER's research director, and in 1957, he became its president. It was through the programs and publications of the NBER, and his speeches to business groups as an NBER executive, that he became well enough known in the corporate community to be invited onto the board of a top-level insurance company.

Not all the Jewish advisers on corporate boards are economists. Daniel Yankelovich, who does attitude surveys and marketing research, received his B.A. and M.A. from Harvard in psychology before joining a market research firm in the early 1950s. In 1958, he formed his own firm, and in 1969, he moved onto a faster track by merging that firm into an acquisition-conscious computer leasing and consulting firm, Leasco, that was headed by entrepreneur Saul Steinberg. Survey-based books on *The Changing Values on Campus* (1973) and *The New Morality* (1974) brought further visibility to Yankelovich. In 1975, he joined with Wall Street lawyer Cyrus Vance in starting an organization called Public Agenda Foundation that was supposed to bring important issues to the attention of the general public, but which also brought attention to Yankelovich and Vance in the process. And in the same year, he joined the board of a major communications corporation, Meredith Corporation (among *Fortune's* second 500 in 1981). Its best-known product is the magazine *Better Homes and Gardens*, but it also owns other magazines as well as book publishing companies and radio and television stations. As an expert on attitudes and marketing, Yankelovich was a natural for this board.

The expert adviser pathway into the boardroom will never be a large one, but it will be steady, and it should remain one that is relevant to Jews, who are a large minority within many academic specializations (Steinberg, 1974).

Ornaments and Tokens

Some directors seem to be chosen for the luster they add to a corporation. Due to past success, especially in government, such people can open doors that might not otherwise be opened. These people are the ornaments on a corporate board.

Former President Gerald Ford seems to be this kind of director. In 1979, he joined his first board, the Pebble Beach Corporation, a resort and real estate subsidiary of Twentieth Century Fox. From that point, the boards came thick and fast—Tiger International, Sante Fe International, Amax, and GK Technologies. In July, 1981, shortly after Jewish oil centimillionaire Marvin Davis of Denver purchased Twentieth Century

Fox for $724 million, he asked his longtime friend Gerald Ford to join that board too.

If someone such as Gerald Ford is primarily an ornament for these several major corporations, others of less fame are their tokens, people chosen because they are women or belong to other minorities. Such people often are asked to be on numerous boards. Indeed, several of the small number of people who sit on four or more corporate boards are in one of the token categories, suggesting that only a relative handful of people performs this function.

Marian Sulzberger Heiskell suspects that she is a token woman on several boards, but such is not the case for the first board she joined. The Sulzbergers on her father's side, and the Ochs on her mother's side, both of German-Jewish ancestry, were the major architects in what journalist David Halberstam (1979: 208) calls "the Ochs-Sulzberger newspaper dynasty," the most famous component of which is *The New York Times*, on whose board she has served since 1963. More recently, she has become the only woman on the boards of Consolidated Edison (the 8th largest utility in 1981), Ford Motor, and Merck (#142).

She was asked to join the Ford board, she told us, "because I was on other boards at the time, word gets around, and I was at the right place at the right time." She thinks she was chosen for these boards because she is a woman, but she said one of her friends made her have second thoughts on the matter. Shortly after she joined Merck's board, the friend asked her why they had chosen her, and she said, "How come? Easy. I'm a woman." Her friend replied: "Don't be so sure that's the only reason. You're also a Jew."

Heiskell does not see any meaningful changes taking place in the makeup of the boards on which she serves. She has at times suggested the names of women, but they have not been chosen as directors. She told us: "I don't see any movement toward more than one woman, or for that matter, more than one black, on a board. As far as tokenism goes, we still have it."

It is unclear if there really are many Jewish tokens, but there are surely some. And, Jewish tokenism is certainly suspected by some of those we spoke with who are the only Jewish members of corporate boards. In fact, one of the men we interviewed, who is the only Jewish member of three different boards, suggested that we speak to the heads of companies with only one Jewish director to see if the Jews had been selected as tokens. Another, Sam Stroum of Seattle, chairman of the board of Schuck's Auto Supply (a 51-store retail auto supply chain in Washington, Oregon, and Idaho), said it was a "total surprise" when he was asked in 1975 to join the board of Seafirst Corporation, the largest bank in the state of Washington and the 26th largest bank in the nation in

1981. He did not know exactly why he had been selected, but he told us that his "gut feeling" was that the board had developed enough sensitivity to seek out "someone highly visible" in the Jewish community. Stroum, who had been active in the Seattle Jewish community for many years, serving at various times as president of his temple and of the Jewish Federation of Greater Seattle, may have been that someone. In any event, no other Jews have been invited to join the board.

It seems unlikely that very many Jews will be asked to join boards as tokens in the future, if they ever have arrived by that route. Jews are not perceived as an unjustly treated minority in America, but as a group that has made it. It is likely that the token positions will be used by corporate leaders in an attempt to pacify other groups that face more blatant barriers.

A NONPATHWAY TO THE TOP:
CLIMBING THE CORPORATE LADDER

Most directors reach the corporate boardroom through a 20- to 30-year climb up the management hierarchy in corporations that their families do not own. True, many of them have a head-start on the average American in terms of family income and educational background, but their rise from that point is a matter of skill, luck, and newly formed social contacts. Once they reach the top in their home corporations, they usually are asked to join the boards of two or three others. It is standard lore in the corporate community that fellow chief executives make fine outside directors because they know the kinds of problems that face a top leader.

This typical pathway is the one that is least open to Jews. In our studies of AJC governors, social club members, and foundation trustees, we were unable to find examples of Jewish executives who had started at the lower rungs of management in a large non-Jewish corporation and worked their way to the top over the usual time period. When we asked about this pathway in our interviews, a few people were able to think of an example or two after some effort, but most couldn't think of any. Moreover, most of the examples suggested in fact had followed somewhat more unconventional paths.

W. Michael Blumenthal, who was born in Germany in 1926 and escaped with his family through Shanghai before coming to the United States in 1947, became president of Bendix Corporation in 1967 and chairman in 1972; he left to serve as President Carter's Secretary of Treasury in 1977. Blumenthal, however, had not worked his way up in Bendix. After receiving his Ph.D. in economics in 1956 at Princeton, he worked for two years as a labor arbitrator for the state of New Jersey and then became a vice president at Crown Cork International. He stayed at Crown Cork until 1961, when he joined the Kennedy administration as a deputy assistant secretary of state for economic affairs and became involved in highly complex tariff negotiations between the United States and West European countries. Then, from 1963 to 1967, Blumenthal served as the President's deputy special representative for trade negotiations, and it was from this position that he moved in at the presidential level at Bendix. (When Blumenthal left the Carter administration in 1979, he became vice-chairman at Burroughs, and, in late 1980, became its chairman and chief executive officer.)

Richard Gelb became president of Bristol-Meyers in 1967 and its chief executive officer shortly thereafter. He then joined the boards of Bankers Trust, Charter Corporation, Cluett Peabody, and *The New York Times*. Gelb did climb the ladder to some degree at Bristol-Meyers, but he started at a very high level; he was president of his family's company, Clairol, when it became a subsidiary of Bristol-Meyers in 1959, and he joined the board of the parent company in 1960. In 1965, at the age of 45, he became Bristol-Meyers' executive vice-president, moving up to the presidency two years later.

The most prominent and visible Jewish chief executive of a non-Jewish corporation in recent years, Irving Shapiro of DuPont, did in fact work for DuPont for 23 years before becoming its chairman and chief executive officer in 1974. However, the circumstances of his employment are once again rather atypical.

In 1949, the federal government initiated an antitrust suit against Christiana Securities, the holding-company subsidiary of the DuPont Corporation through which the duPont family controlled the corporation. The suit claimed that Christiana Securities owned a significant amount of stock in General Motors, and that this stock was used to dominate that company, giving DuPont "an illegal preference over its competition in the sale of paint, chemicals, and other products to GM" (Goulden, 1973: 99). The suit was to drag on for a decade, twice going before the Supreme Court before the family and the corporation finally lost and Christiana Securities was ordered to get rid of all General Motors stock within ten years.

Even that did not end the matter, however. The duPonts argued with Justice, Treasury, and the Internal Revenue Service over how the divestiture should take place, and what the tax consequences should be. The whole matter was not settled until DuPont Corporation lawyers, with the help of New York and Washington corporate lawyers, were able to convince Congress to pass a special law for the benefit of DuPont stockholders.

Two years after this extremely complex saga began, DuPont hired Shapiro, then a government lawyer, to help with the case even though he had no experience with antitrust law. A 1941 graduate of the law school at the University of Minnesota, he had worked for a year at the Office of Price Administration in Washington before switching over to the Justice Department, where he spent eight years as a prosecuting attorney. Shapiro first made a name for himself by arguing and winning a case that extended federal jurisdiction in the area of civil rights, and he then became the successful prosecutor in one of the most controversial cases of the late 1940s—the trial of 11 leaders of the Communist Party on charges of advocating the overthrow of the government.

Shapiro spent two full years with dozens of other DuPont lawyers helping to prepare for the antitrust case, but he was left behind at company headquarters in Delaware when the 110-person legal team went to Chicago to begin the actual trial in 1953. He remained in Delaware because he had been chosen to be the liaison between the legal staff and top management, interpreting the legal arguments to the executives and explaining the alternative strategies open to them. It was this assignment that brought him to the attention of the chief executives and opened up the possibility of his movement into management ranks.

After the case was lost in the courts, Shapiro was among the small group of lawyers inside and outside the company that worked out the deal in Washington for the divestiture. The duPonts and their corporation faced the following dilemma. If they sold the stock on the open market, it might depress the price of the stock, or so they argued. If they distributed the GM stock to DuPont's own shareholders, who were in good part wealthy members of the duPont family, the distributed stock would be taxed as "ordinary income," meaning that the tax rate would be in a very high bracket.

The duPonts took their problem to a Washington lawyer, Clark Clifford, for advice. His solution was to write a special tax bill that would allow the duPonts to pay taxes as if the distributed stock were a capital gain; the result was that the maximum tax rate on the increase in the value of the stock since it was first issued many years before would be only 25 percent. This bill, which Shapiro helped to shepherd through Congress, reduced the tax liability from approximately $45.00 per share to about $7.25 per share, thereby saving the duPonts several million dollars in taxes (Goulden, 1973: 99–102).

For his work on the case, both within the company and with the government, Shapiro was named assistant general counsel in 1965. It became his ambition to rise to the top of the legal department, but to his surprise he was named a vice president and director in 1970, putting him in line as a possible chief executive officer. His handling of a group of

Nader's Raiders who came to Delaware to investigate the DuPont Corporation increased his stature even further, and in 1972, he became a senior vice president. In 1974, he was named chairman and chief executive officer, a position he held until his retirement at age 65 in 1981.

Once in the top position, Shapiro was, like other chief executive officers, asked to join several boards, and accepted offers to join those of IBM, Citicorp, and Continental Assurance. He became a member of the most visible and successful business lobbying group, the Business Roundtable, and served as its chairman from 1976 to 1978, a position from which he developed a close relationship with his fellow Democrat in the White House, Jimmy Carter.

Shapiro told us he doubts that "my religion had anything to do with my job pro or con. I think it had to do with circumstances, people and so on." As he told another interviewer, his most important asset was his ability to deal with government, a quality that often had been lacking in the past in the highly conservative DuPont hierarchy (Taylor, 1979: 17).

The careers of men such as Blumenthal, Gelb, and Shapiro suggest that non-Jewish business leaders are willing to promote Jewish executives within their corporations once these men have proven themselves. However, it also seems to be the case that few Jews have been able to start at the bottom and prove themselves in the usual ways. Climbing the corporate ladder still remains somewhat problematic for Jews.

CONCLUSION

Previous studies and our own research demonstrate that Jews are part of the corporate elite in representative numbers, but it is equally apparent that, with a few exceptions, they are on the periphery of this elite. They are not even remotely close to being the dominant force they are tragically and mistakenly thought to be by anti-Semites. Moreover, one of the most important pathways into this elite remains, in good part, blocked for Jews at its lower rungs, a finding which leads us to Baltzell's claim that social clubs play a key role in the advancement of corporate executives. It is time to see how successful Jewish businessmen and their families fare within the clubs and other institutions of the social elite.

Chapter 3

Jews
in
the Social Elite

In this chapter we will switch our focus from the corporate elite to the social elite. We will investigate three different institutions, looking in each case at both the frequency of Jewish involvement and the nature of that involvement. First, we will consider private clubs. Have Jews become members of the "top" clubs in America? To the extent that they have, how do those Jews who have joined such clubs differ from those who have not? And have the much publicized discriminatory policies of certain clubs affected the professional lives of Jewish businessmen?

Second, we will look at institutions that have significant social clout, though, unlike social clubs, they do not purport to be primarily social in nature. These are the private secondary schools, sometimes called prep schools, or boarding schools if the students live on campus. We will discuss the role of these institutions in preparing young people, especially young men, for adult life in the upper class.

Finally, we will turn to yet another institution that allows for social interaction between upper-class gentiles and upper-class Jews, though it too, like the prep school, does not define itself primarily in social terms. We are referring to the boards of a city's major cultural institutions, such as museums and the opera, where corporate leaders (and, frequently, their wives) meet regularly in their efforts to provide enriching cultural experiences for themselves and other people in their cities. We will examine the cultural elites of the three largest cities in America: New York, Los Angeles, and Chicago.

THE SOCIAL CLUB

There has been a great deal written about "gentlemanly" anti-Semitism in upper-class clubs. Baltzell, in dealing with this subject,

47

referred to it as "among the sorriest symbols of discrimination in America" (1964: 357). He documents the fact that, as of the early 1960s, many of the most prestigious clubs in America routinely excluded Jews from membership. One of the many examples he cited was that of Pittsburgh's Duquesne Club, which, he wrote, "lies at the very core of the associational organization of leadership in Pittsburgh." Another was New York's Links Club, which Baltzell referred to as "the New York rendezvous of the national corporate establishment."

In addition to the obvious social discrimination when Jews are barred from membership in such clubs as the Duquesne and the Links, Baltzell argued that there is an accompanying effect on the professional lives of those who are discriminated against. Because so much business allegedly is done at these "social" clubs, and because Jews are unable to engage in such business at those clubs that exclude them, corporations are said to be reluctant to promote Jews to upper-level executive positions. As Baltzell put it: "In city after city, the admissions policies of the top clubs are increasingly causing our national corporations to bar some of their best-qualified men from top leadership positions." In his phrase, the club is the tail that wags the corporate dog (1964: 362).

Sociologist Reed Powell, in a study sponsored by the American Jewish Committee as part of its program to remove discriminatory barriers at social clubs for all religious and ethnic minorities, provided interview evidence that supports Baltzell's contentions. After talking with several hundred West Coast executives and obtaining their reactions to a series of short questions, Powell concluded that clubs are an important element in gaining promotions for executives within American corporations. He found clubs to be places where views are presented, ideas are modified, and some business is informally transacted. Furthermore, clubs are one setting in which rising executives are socialized into the values of the social elite: "The clubs are a repository of the values held by the upper-level prestige groups in the community and are a means by which these values are transferred to the business environment" (Powell, 1969: 50).

More recently, attacks on the exclusionary policies of these clubs have been expanded to include the barring of women. When the Committee on Banking, Housing, and Urban Affairs of the United States Senate considered the question of whether corporations should pay the membership fees and dues to clubs that have discriminatory admissions policies, in addition to two witnesses from the American Jewish Committee and one from the Anti-Defamation League of B'nai B'rith, there was a witness representing the Women's Equity Action League (U.S. Senate, 1978). Because the average country club would lose over $300,000 annually and the average city club would lose about $450,000 annually if corporations were barred from making such payments, many clubs are getting very nervous (*Business Week*, 1980: 40). Some have even taken in women members.

We began our inquiry into the involvement of Jews in top social clubs with the list developed by Domhoff (1970) that was mentioned in the first chapter as one aspect of our operational definition of the social elite. This list, which appears in Table 3.1, includes 40 clubs from all parts of the country, but does not include clubs from every major city. Using the biographical information that we accumulated on the Jewish corporate directors, club members and foundation trustees described in the last chapter, and by looking at past and current membership lists for some of these clubs, we found that there are far fewer Jews in elite clubs than on *Fortune*-level corporate boards.

Of the more than 4,000 Jews we have identified as either members of AJC's Board of Governors, the Harmonie or Standard Clubs, or as philanthropists included in the *Trustees of Wealth*, we have been able to find only 24 who are members of one or more of the top-level clubs. In the case

TABLE 3.1.
Clubs in the Social Elite

Arlington (Portland, Ore.)	Maryland (Baltimore)
Boston (New Orleans)	Milwaukee (Milwaukee)
Brook (New York)	Minneapolis (Minneapolis)
Burlingame Country Club (San Francisco)	New Haven Lawn Club (New Haven)
California (Los Angeles)	Pacific Union (San Francisco)
Casino (Chicago)	Philadelphia (Philadelphia)
Century (New York)	Piedmont Driving (Atlanta)
Chagrin Valley Hunt (Cleveland)	Piping Rock (New York)
Charleston (Charleston, S.C.)	Racquet Club (St. Louis)
Chicago (Chicago)	Rainier (Seattle)
Cuyamuca (San Diego)	Richmond German (Richmond)
Denver (Denver)	Rittenhouse (Philadelphia)
Detroit (Detroit)	River (New York)
Eagle Lake (Houston)	Rolling Rock (Pittsburgh)
Everglades (Palm Beach)	Saturn (Buffalo)
Hartford (Hartford, Conn.)	St. Cecelia (Charleston, S.C.)
Hope (Providence)	St. Louis Country Club (St. Louis)
Idlewild (Dallas)	Somerest (Boston)
Knickerbocker (New York)	Union (Cleveland)
Links (New York)	Woodhill Country Club (Minneapolis)

of the foundation trustees, where we can compare the number of Jews who are members of these clubs with a matched group of non-Jewish trustees, the difference is striking: only 12 of the Jewish trustees were in one or more of these clubs, as compared to 47 of the non-Jewish trustees.

These findings on the relatively small number of Jews in elite clubs were corroborated by a survey we did in the late 1970s (Zweigenhaft, 1980: 63–65). We wrote to the 25 regional directors of the American Jewish Committee, and the 19 regional directors of the American Jewish Congress. In response to questions about the admissions practices of clubs in their geographical areas, we found that some clubs in some cities had taken in Jewish members, but typically these were not the most prestigious clubs. Of the 11 clubs on our list that were included in the information we received from our respondents, 4 had taken in Jewish members: the Chicago Club was estimated at that time to have between 6 and 15 Jewish members; the Detroit Club was estimated to have at least 6 Jewish members; Los Angeles' California Club was thought to have between 1 and 3 Jewish members; and Seattle's Rainier Club was thought to have between 6 and 8. In contrast, the following seven clubs were thought at that time to have no Jewish members: Atlanta's Piedmont Driving Club; Chicago's Casino Club; Houston's Eagle Lake; Milwaukee's Milwaukee Club; Philadelphia's Philadelphia Club; Pittsburgh's Rolling Rock; and St. Louis' St. Louis Country Club.

The city with the least exclusionary record on social clubs appears to be Cincinnati. Its downtown men's club, the Queen City, which is not on our list, has been open to Jewish members for at least 25 years, according to Herbert R. Bloch, Jr., a former department store executive in that city who is now president of Bullock's in Los Angeles. "While I do not have an accurate count, I would judge the Jewish membership in the Queen City is between three and five percent of the total," said Bloch. The uniqueness of the situation in Cincinnati is attested to by Seymour Brief, the executive director of the American Jewish Committee for the Ohio–Kentucky area. He thinks that city "does indeed have more open club policies than any other city, at least in the case of Jews," and he guesses that this is due to the fact that "a great many members of the Jewish community in Cincinnati go back two, three, and even four generations." Then too, Cincinnati did not have a very great influx of Eastern European Jews, so the older relationship between gentiles and the German Jews was not as threatened there as it was in many other cities.

Another dramatic exception to the general questionnaire findings was discovered in an interview with Samuel Maslon, a Minneapolis lawyer who until 1976 sat on the board of North Central Airlines (the 48th largest transportation company for that year). After answering our questions, Maslon suggested we talk with Martin Borman, a graduate of Harvard Law School who had joined Maslon's firm in the late 1940s. In that interview, we learned that there has been a radical change in recent years in the club situation in Minneapolis, a city that had been notable earlier in the century for having a considerable amount of anti-Semitism (Higham, 1975: 163). In fact, one of the directors we spoke with told us that when he finished law school at the University of Minnesota in the 1930s, he was advised that if he wanted to succeed as a lawyer in Minneapolis he would have to change his name to one that sounded less Jewish. Not very long ago, there were no Jewish members of the prestigious Minneapolis Club, and those Jews who sought membership in such a club joined Minneapolis' Standard Club (a Jewish club). By 1981, there were about 100 Jewish members of the Minneapolis Club (out of a total membership of about 1,000), the Standard Club had folded, and the Minneapolis Club had elected Martin Borman as its first Jewish president.

More typical than the situations we have described in Cincinnati and Minneapolis, however, has been the case of the California Club in Los Angeles. As of the late 1960s, there were no Jews among the club's 1,200 members (though some of its founders back in 1888 had been Jewish). The American Jewish Committee had been conducting a campaign for ten years to break down the barriers to this and other clubs, but had worked exclusively behind the scenes. As Neil C. Sandburg, the regional director of the AJC said of their efforts in Los Angeles, "We've been working on the problem here for 10 years, and have not said one word publicly. We felt it would be more constructive, more useful, more harmonious in terms of good community relationships if we could effect change quietly" (Los Angeles Times, July 3, 1969: 19).

There had been many "quiet protests," some by members of the AJC and some by others, but these had no observable impact on the admissions policies of the California Club. AJC member Martin Gang, a prominent Los Angeles attorney, said he had "run up against a stone wall" in trying to discuss the issue with top officers of the club.

When one of the directors we spoke with in Los Angeles, Sidney Brody, became a member of the board of the Civic Light Opera in the mid-1960s, that board held its meetings at the California Club, and Brody refused to meet there: "I said that I wouldn't meet there because I didn't want to go any place as a guest that I wasn't welcome as a member, so we changed the meeting place." Similarly, when State Supreme Court Justice Stanley Mosk was informed that his speech to the University Club, scheduled to take place at the California Club, would not be attended by certain Jewish members of the University Club because of the exclusionary policies of the California Club, Mosk decided to proceed with his

speech but referred directly to those not in attendance, and told his audience: "I hope you will consider thoughtfully before future meetings are held in this building."

In July, 1969, however, the AJC brought its campaign into the open with the publication of a seven-year study done under its sponsorship by sociologist Reed Powell. The 450-page report catalogued in detail the frequency and impact of club discrimination against Jews. Sandburg explained the decision to "bring the campaign into the open," in the following way: "We've reached the point where they told us, our friends in these clubs, 'Fire your best shots.' That's a quote from a former president of the California Club" (*Los Angeles Times*, July 3, 1969: 19).

It was in the context of such heightened awareness of the issue that an individual of Jewish background was nominated to the California Club in August, 1974. Franklin Murphy, the chairman of the board of Times Mirror, and a member of the California Club, nominated Harold Brown, a noted physicist, an official in the Department of Defense during the Vietnam era, and then the president of the California Institute of Technology. A number of years earlier, Brown had been proposed, but the club had never acted on the nomination. This time, the nomination was not acted upon for more than two years, until Murphy and the Jewish Federation Council began to take actions. In late 1976, while Murphy arranged meetings with various officers and leaders in the club, the Federation Council mailed letters to the chief executives of 160 major corporations in Southern California, urging them to express opposition to the California Club's discriminatory policies, not to hold meetings there, and not to pay their employees' membership dues at that club. Then, in mid-November, after Jimmy Carter had been elected President, it was rumored that Harold Brown was being considered as Secretary of Defense. Suddenly, in late November, the club decided to take in its first Jewish member since the turn of the century (*Los Angeles Times*, December 6, 1976: 1, 8–10). One of the men we interviewed described Brown's ground-breaking acceptance into the club as a "tortuous process in which a lot of his friends expended a lot of energy propelling him along." The relation of his acceptance to his appointment as Secretary of Defense may or may not have been coincidence.

Since that time, the California Club has taken in between five and ten Jewish members, including former ambassador and media magnate Walter Annenberg, who just a few years earlier, had been blackballed by the Philadelphia Club (Cooney, 1982: 380). But there is a much lower percentage of Jews in the California Club than in the Los Angeles corporate elite.

In general, it is safe to conclude that Jews have become a much more significant part of the national corporate elite than of the social elite, at least as far as the top social clubs comprise the social elite. How can this be if, as Baltzell has asserted, it is the social club that is the tail that wags the corporate dog? Before we try to answer this question, let us look more carefully at which Jews do and do not become members of the clubs we have been considering.

Who Joins?

The first, and most obvious, characteristic of the men who join these clubs is that many of them are on major corporate boards. Of the 24 men we have identified in one or more clubs on our list, 9 sit on *Fortune*-level boards, and 6 of those sit on more than one such board. Of our club members, the most impressive list of corporate directorships was held by John M. Schiff, the former Kuhn, Loeb partner who sat on six boards.

Another striking characteristic of this group of men is that almost all of them (21 of 24) received their undergraduate education at one of the elite private universities that account for 54 percent of all private endowment funds in higher education (Dye, 1979: 133–34). Fourteen of them received their undergraduate education at Ivy League colleges (six at Yale, two at Cornell, two at Princeton, three at Harvard, and one at the University of Pennsylvania), and four of the others went to Ivy League schools for postgraduate degrees (two to Harvard, one to Yale, and one to Columbia). Graduation from Ivy League or other prestigious colleges is not simply evidence that these men received "proper" educations, including the opportunity to meet upper-class gentiles who were later to populate the clubs; it also suggests they came from families that were well enough established economically to afford such expensive educations. There were few scholarships in the period when these men went to school and, according to Baltzell (1976: 505), "a large proportion of the scholarships at boarding schools and prestige colleges went to the sons of impecunious genteel, rather than the sons of underprivileged ethnic and minority groups."

There is yet another way that elite club members differed from nonmembers: They were more likely to be from German-Jewish immigrant families than from Eastern European immigrant families. For the most part, as already noted, the divisions within the Jewish community between German and Eastern Jews ceased long ago. Clubs like the Harmonie and the Standard, once exclusive domains of German Jews, took successful Eastern Jews into their ranks decades ago. Similarly, a prestigious organization such as the American Jewish Committee, once dominated by German Jews, now has many Eastern European Jews in its membership and in its leadership (as one long-time AJC member told us, "Nobody asks and nobody cares"). And, of course, as more and more German Jews married Eastern European Jews, such distinctions became less and less meaningful. Inland Steel's Joseph Block, from an old-line German Jewish family, explained it this way: "There got to be so much intermarriage that those lines disappeared. Both my sisters married Eastern Jews."

Yet, when it came to membership in upper-class gentile clubs, there were clear differences between German and most Eastern Jews. Most of the German Jews we interviewed had been one of the first, and often the only, Jewish member of a gentile club. When F. Warren Hellman, whose German-born great-grandfather had become president of Wells Fargo Bank in 1905, was in New York as a partner in Lehman Brothers, he was one of the few Jewish members of Long Island's Piping Rock Country Club. San Franciscans Walter and Peter Haas, of Levi Strauss (and, between them, half a dozen other *Fortune*-level boards), were two of the first four members of the Pacific Union Club, and Walter was the first Jewish member of the Bohemian Club since early in the century. Joseph Block was not only one of the first two Jews to join the Chicago Club; when in Washington during World War II he had been the only Jewish member of the formerly (and subsequently) restricted Congressional Country Club. When a group of his fellow steel executives (all gentiles) who were working with him in the steel division of the War Production Board came to him and said they wanted to join Congressional, and that they would not join unless he did, he became the first and only Jewish member. Congressional apparently was willing to waive the restriction as a patriotic gesture, but only during war-time conditions. After the war, when Block returned to Chicago, the club returned to its former policy.

Furthermore, when we asked the German-Jewish corporate directors if they would have accepted had they been asked to join by a prestigious club such as New York's Links or Knickerbocker, all indicated that they at least would have considered it. In fact, some of the German-Jewish directors were quite aware that they had not been asked into these clubs. As Joseph F. Cullman pointed out: "I am on some pretty good boards, as you can see. It would have been normal with the connections I've got to have been asked to have joined one of those clubs, but I wasn't. And, you know, I survived very well without it. But I can recall it. It didn't go unnoticed."

The corporate directors of Eastern European background responded quite differently. Without exception, they made it clear that they were not interested in being the only Jewish member of a gentile club. The comment of Irving Rabb, Vice Chairman of the Board of Stop and Shop, was not atypical: "I wouldn't accept a membership in one of these clubs unless it was open, and a whole bunch of Jews were there." Corporate lawyer Simon Rifkind had a similar reaction:

> When I left Columbia I refused to join the Columbia Club because it was tendered to me as "You're the one." I said "Nothing doing." And I'm glad to see they collapsed . . . I can only speak for myself. If I were one of one or two Jews at a club, and somebody voted for me because I was the richest man in town . . . or something like that, I would not join. If, on the other hand, I had the impression that the club had become civilized, I might very well join.

Laurence Tisch, Chairman of the Board at Loews, was even more direct when asked the same question: "Never had any interest. Naa. I think it's very unimportant whether they take Jewish members or they don't take Jewish members. I don't think it's good for the Jews, because I think all you do is end up diluting your own background and your own values and you try to imitate their values, and I have no desire to do that."

Differences between successful German-Jewish and Eastern European Jewish corporate directors are also differences between old and new money. The few exceptions to the pattern we have just described help make this clear. The only Jewish member of the prestigious Links Club whom we have discovered in our research is CBS's William Paley, the grandson of a Russian Jew. But unlike so many other Russian Jews, described by Birmingham (1967: 289) as "ragged, dirt-poor," and "toughened by years of torment," Paley's grandfather had been the Czar's representative in his town, and came to America in style. Paley describes his grandfather's arrival in his autobiography, *As It Happened* (1979: 5):

> Grandfather Isaac thought that the time had come when emigration might be a wise course for the family. With permission to travel and also the wherewithal, as the owner of a prospering lumber business, he made a voyage to America, around 1883–84, taking his nine-year-old son, my father, to visit and see if he liked it. He did like it, returned to Russia, and apparently made plans. Four years later he moved everyone to Chicago. The entourage was considerable: himself; his wife, Zelda; my father, who was then thirteen; three other sons—William, Jacob and Benjamin; and three daughters, Sophie, Sarah and Celia.

Lester Crown, one of the few Jews in the Chicago Club of eastern descent, is also the grandchild of a very early Eastern European immigrant—his grandfather came from Latvia in the 1860s, and by Lester's childhood, the Crown family was a financial force to be reckoned with in Chicago.

On the 42nd floor of Rockefeller Plaza, with a spectacular view north over Central Park, we spoke with another man whose unusual background helped shed light on this difference between new and old money. Significantly, he is neither of Eastern European nor of German heritage. Ezra Zilkha was born in Baghdad to a family with a long history in the Middle Eastern economic elite. His father's bank was the largest privately owned commercial bank in the Arab world, and there is a Zilkha synagogue in Baghdad that was built in the thirteenth century. At the time of our interview, Zilkha was the only Jew on the boards of INA (the 7th largest diversified financial company in America in 1981) and Handy & Harmon (the 360th largest industrial), and was also one of very few Jews who is a member of New York's exclusive Knicker-bocker Club.

Zilkha spent the highly important formative years of his life in Lebanon and Egypt, where he learned to speak Arabic, English, and French fluently. As he said: "Don't forget I'm a Baghdad Jew. In the middle east, the stratification had nothing to do with religion. It had to do with social background, it had to do with family background, and it had to do with wealth." When he came to America in 1941 at the age of 16, he was enrolled at the prestigious Hill School, where he made life-long friends. Years later, through the efforts of one of his Hill School class-mates, the Zilkhas were to become the first Jewish family to join the Meadow Club in Southampton. In addition to his memberships in the Knickerbocker Club and the Meadow Club, he has been a member of the Brooks in London, the Traveller's and Polo Clubs in Paris, and has been a guest at the Bohemian Grove in northern California.

Zilkha, impeccably tailored and with the manner and bearing of an international aristocrat, is comfortable interacting with members of the corporate and social elite around the world, and unlike many of the German Jews we spoke with, he maintains his ties to Judaism. He is a member of a Sephardic congregation in New York, and his involvement entails more than merely paying membership fees: "I go four times a year. I go for my father's yahrzeit [the anniversary of a relative's death], my brother's yahrzeit, Yom Kippur and Rosh Hashonah. I contribute to the synagogue because that's where I was married, that's where my son was bar-mitzvahed, and the synagogue arranged the burial of my father and brother. This is part of my family life." In addition, Zilkha has given money to Princeton University to be used for the study of the history of Jews in the Near East. Zilkha's continued personal commitment to Jewish ritual and his strong sense of Jewish identity suggest that when people's families have been part of the upper class for centuries, rather than two or three generations, they may not feel anxious about retaining their Jewish identity.

It is clear, then, that there aren't many Jewish members in America's most prestigious clubs, and that those who are members are from families that achieved economic success at least a generation ago, and often earlier. For the most part, these are German Jews, but, as we have indicated, there are a few grandsons of Eastern European Jews who arrived early enough for them to have grown up with the economic comfort that makes them acceptable to, and interested in, the best clubs. As one director we spoke with put it: "It's really the difference between John Schiff and Larry Tisch, for instance. There is a difference. I mean, John Schiff is carrying the past, and Larry Tisch, thirty years ago, nobody ever heard of. I know them both and I admire them both."

In returning to the question of whether or not these clubs are the "tails that wag the corporate dog," let us consider the case of the son of a Lithuanian Jew who surprised everyone, including himself, by emerging as the chief executive officer of a non-Jewish corporation even though he wasn't in any of the right clubs.

In 1974, DuPont Corporation broke new ground within the corporate community with the announcement that its next chairman of the board was to be Irving S. Shapiro, a lawyer, a non-duPont, and a Jew. Shapiro's predecessor, C. B. McCoy, was the only other chief executive who had not been a member of the duPont family, and McCoy was a second generation higher executive within the company whose family, according to the *Wall Street Journal* (1975: 1), was "closely linked to the duPonts in a variety of ways." The *Wall Street Journal* accordingly broke the news to its readership with a headline that read: "Breaking the Mold: Boss-to-Be at DuPont Is an Immigrant's Son Who Climbed Hard Way."

One of the surprises about Shapiro's appointment noted by financial observers was that he was not a member of the "right" clubs. The *Wall Street Journal* article just referred to pointed out that he was not only "a lawyer in a company traditionally run by financial and technical men," but that he was "a Jew who doesn't belong to all the right clubs." It did not take long, however, for the clubs to approach Shapiro. He was asked to join various clubs in the Wilmington area that previously had shown no interest in having him, or anyone else who was Jewish, as a member. His explanation of how he decided which ones to join, and not join, certainly is what we would have predicted for a second-generation Eastern European Jew whose father had to struggle to afford paying for his education at the state university:

As soon as my designation to this position was announced I was invited to join one of the local country clubs that until then made it a practice not to admit Jews, and I simply declined the invitation. That created consternation because other clubs were in the process of clearing the decks to invite me. Some of the people here were concerned with that, were fearful that if I turned them down, too, it might present a problem. The line I drew is very simple, I'll do whatever is appropriate that relates to our business interests—a downtown club is that kind of thing. A country club, on the other hand, is related to my personal activities, and I didn't see any need for my joining, accepting the offer that was made in a place where I wouldn't have been welcome a month earlier.

As for the city club, Shapiro made it clear that he would join only with the agreement that other Jews would become members as well, because, as he put it, "It would be intolerable for me to be the only one."

It is our belief that Baltzell's claim, further articulated by Powell and various spokesmen for Jewish groups, that the exclusionary policies of clubs have prevented Jewish businessmen from rising through the corporate ranks, is not false, but does oversimplify a more complex relationship between clubs and corporations. Though we have demonstrated that many Jewish businessmen are directors of *Fortune*-level corporations, but very few of them have been accepted into the "best" clubs, we have also demonstrated that there are various pathways to the top. Many of the Jewish corporate directors we identified have traveled a pathway into the corporate elite in which they emerged as directors on the boards of companies founded or taken over by Jewish families (in some cases, their own families). In such corporations, a young Jewish executive attempting to rise through the ranks was neither required nor expected to be a member of clubs that discriminated against Jews. Lester Crown did not have to become a member of the Chicago Club to rise in the corporate world, though he did in fact become a member of that club in the late 1970s. Similarly, Maynard Wishner, who joined Walter E. Heller in 1963, became a director a few years later and became president in 1974, was not required to be a member of any clubs that discriminated against Jews because Walter Heller, the company's founder, was Jewish (Wishner is not in the Chicago Club, nor is he in the Standard Club; however, since 1977 he has been the chairman of the American Jewish Committee's board of governors). In such cases, it could be said, the gentile club has not wagged the tail of the Jewish corporations.

The same conclusion could be drawn for two other pathways we described as routes to the corporate elite, those of the investment banker and of the corporate lawyer. Traditionally, such people have been asked to join corporate boards as financial and legal advisers, and this has been true for Jewish as well as gentile investment bankers. Jewish partners at Goldman, Sachs or other investment houses have not been kept out of the corporate elite just because they have been excluded from certain clubs. Former Lehman Brothers partner F. Warren Hellman explains it this way: "There were a lot of Lehman partners who were Jewish who were on very important boards. If they weren't Jewish, and they were important guys, they were on more boards. It's kind of a relative thing." It is perhaps true that Jewish investment bankers and lawyers have been somewhat more likely to be asked to join the boards of Jewish corporations than non-Jewish corporations, but as we have shown in the cases of Sidney J. Weinberg and Ford, and Irving Shapiro and DuPont, there also have been Jewish investment bankers and lawyers on corporations that were not founded by Jews. Although Weinberg was on the Ford board, he never was asked to join "top-flight clubs" like the Links or the Knickerbocker (Baltzell, 1964: 36).

It is those individuals who have tried to move up through the ranks in non-Jewish corporations who have had the most difficulty, and may have been affected by the restrictive policies of the clubs. These corporations, as we indicated in the last chapter, include most of the largest in America. Those Jewish directors we have discovered on their boards have been outside rather than inside directors, which means that they made their mark elsewhere (often in a Jewish corporation) and then were asked to join the boards. As far as we have been able to tell, very few have moved up through the corporate ranks.

But have these corporations been pushed around by the clubs in their cities? It is certain that DuPont was not, and it is hard to imagine that corporations such as Exxon, Mobil, and General Motors (to name the top three on *Fortune*'s 1981 list) are at the mercy of clubs. It is easier to believe that these companies have shared the anti-Semitism of the clubs, and used club membership as a convenient criterion for promoting those they wanted to promote. This line of reasoning is even more persuasive when it is recalled that a substantial portion of the membership fees and dues paid to clubs is paid by corporations. The National Club Association, which represents 1,000 of the nation's leading country and city clubs, estimates that a full 37 percent of the income of city clubs comes from "company-paid memberships" (*Business Week*, 1980: 90).

Though we do not have data on this, it is also likely that many ambitious Jewish businessmen have seen the writing on the wall and avoided this particular path to the top. Laurence Tisch, acknowledging that discrimination in clubs contributes to discrimination in corporations, says the answer is not to join the clubs but to avoid the corporations: "I think in America so much depends on social acquaintances for advancement in the business world, especially in the so-called structured business world—the insurance companies, the utilities or the major corporations—that if you're not able to join clubs it's more difficult to advance. But I don't think that's important at all for Jews. I think in a way the Jews are better off not being in these big corporations because all they'll do is get bogged down."

Whether Irving Shapiro's emergence as the chief executive at DuPont without having had the proper club credentials has signaled a change in club and corporate policies remains to be seen. Shapiro believes that his selection by DuPont already has affected the decisions made by other corporations, though there had been only one Jew—W. Michael Blumenthal—appointed as the chief executive officer of a major non-Jewish corporation in the eight years between Shapiro's appointment and the time of our interview. He told us of a Jewish executive at a cocktail party telling him that after years of doing business with a bank in Toronto, he had received a call from the president of the bank, who said, "As long as Shapiro's good enough for DuPont, it's about time we put you on our board." This example involves a Canadian bank, but Shapiro stressed that this is but one of many such examples and that American corporations are changing, too.

At the same time, Shapiro is not convinced that those kept out of clubs because of being Jewish have been hampered professionally. He refers to those who make such claims as "second and third raters who use it as a crutch." He does not think that club policies have been particularly important: "I can't say it never happened, but I'd think it was an unusual situation. I simply can't believe that it has kept people down."

Some of the other Jewish directors we spoke with doubted that much business-related activity took place at clubs, but others thought that clubs were for business as well as for social purposes. Furthermore, some noted that even if people engage only in "social talk" at the club, this may yield economic benefits later. Chicago centimillionaire Jay Pritzker pointed out that people like himself who have made it to the top are likely to forget the valuable role that clubs can play: "Having attained the position we have, it's hard to recall the earlier importance of clubs. But, yeah, damn right, being excluded from clubs is a restraint because you don't meet people you need to meet on a social level."

We conclude that limited access to clubs may have contributed to the limited access that various non-whites, non–Anglo-Saxons, non-Protestants, and women have had to the higher echelons of many American corporations, but we would place primary responsibility for such limited access on the corporations themselves. As DuPont has shown, corporations don't need to cater to such club prejudices. Unlike many other minority groups, however, Jews have been able, at least in part, to move around this barrier by traveling other paths to the corporate elite. A young Jewish businessman has had a better chance of becoming a part of the corporate elite if he took Laurence Tisch's advice and avoided large gentile-controlled corporations and either joined a firm Jews had started or, like Tisch, developed his own.

There are two additional places of social interaction that we must consider before leaving our investigation of Jews in the social elite. A look at these two institutions also may help us to see if the role of clubs has been over-emphasized.

PRIVATE SCHOOLS

A graduate of the Lawrenceville School who wrote a book called *The Finest Education Money Can Buy* described his alma mater in the following manner:

> Lawrenceville is one of the country's larger and more venerable prep schools. Founded in 1810 (on money made in the opium trade, according to student lore), it now has an enrollment of about 650 boys (85 percent of whom are boarders) in grades eight through twelve. The school is located on 330 magnificently landscaped acres of New Jersey countryside just five miles south of Princeton. Its physical plant—including a nine-hole golf course, mammoth field house and covered hockey rink, library of some 23,000 volumes, science building, arts center with 900-seat auditorium and professionally equipped stage—would be the envy of most colleges (Gaines, 1972: 10).

It is in such physical surroundings that many children of the upper class receive the educations that prepare them for college—and for life in the corporate and social elite.

Baltzell (1964: 127–8) points out that many prominent American prep schools were established during the period that coincided with what he refers to as "trust-founding" and "trust-busting." As the national upper class grew in the last half of the nineteenth century, so did the desire on the part of its members for schools like Choate, Deerfield, Hotchkiss, Kent, Middlesex, and Taft, all of which were founded within a decade of the turn of the twentieth century (or, in Baltzell's words, "within a decade of the formation of the U.S. Steel Corporation").

These schools, and others like them, provide an opportunity for contact among children of upper-class families from around the country. Some private schools always have had some Jewish students, and, more recently, some have provided scholarships for minority students. Many, like Baltzell, see these developments as evidence that the American Dream still lives. Baltzell writes that "This ethnic aristocracy of talented and ambitious young people now attending . . . such schools as Exeter and Andover (and, to an increasing extent, such schools as Groton and

St. Paul's) provides dramatic witness to the staying power of the American Dream of equality of opportunity" (1964: 345). Others, however, are not similarly persuaded that the addition of minority or working class students at elite schools is evidence of meaningful progress toward true equality of opportunity. Marxist economist Paul Sweezy, himself a graduate of Exeter, claims that social scientists should not be "confused" by the fact that a considerable number of lower-class families succeed in getting their children into prestigious prep schools. The prep schools, he argues, are merely "recruiters for the ruling class, sucking upwards the ablest elements of the lower classes and thus performing the double function of infusing new brains into the ruling class and weakening the political leadership of the working class" (Baltzell, 1964: 344).

Our interest, of course, is in the Jews who have attended such schools and the effect of that experience on them. Although it is more difficult to determine attendance at private schools than membership in clubs because fewer people include them in their *Who's Who in America* biographies (Domhoff, 1970: 31; Useem, personal communication), we have used such information when it appears to gauge the frequency with which successful Jews have attended prep schools. In addition, we have tried to ascertain the nature of their experiences at these schools through our interviews with corporate directors.

We utilized the list of 37 private schools developed by Domhoff (1970) that appears in Table 3.2 for our starting point. We have added Exeter and Andover to his list since he omitted them only because of their "large minority of scholarship students." Twenty-five of the men in our sample, beginning with George Washington Naumberg, who graduated from Exeter in 1894, went to one of these 39 schools.

As was the case with clubs, we also compared the 219 Jews drawn from the *Trustees of Wealth* with the 219 non-Jews from the same source. We found that 17 of the Jewish philanthropists had attended one of the elite prep schools on the list, as compared to 14 of the non-Jews. Similarly, when we compared the 12 Jews in a 1978 Senate subcommittee report on directors on three or more boards with the 55 who specify non-Jewish religions in their *Who's Who in America* biographies (19 Episcopalians, 13 Presbyterians, 7 Roman Catholics, and 16 who list various other Protestant denominations), and with the 141 who do not reveal their religion, we found that the Jewish interlocking directors were as likely to have attended schools on our list as the others (U.S. Senate Committee on Governmental Affairs, 1978). Whereas 7 of the 55 (11.3 percent) who indicated some Protestant or Catholic denomination listed one of the prep schools on our list, and 12 of the 141 (8.5 percent) who gave no indication of their religion did so, 2 of the 12 (16.6 percent) Jews attended schools on the list. The Episcopalians were the only ones to indicate

TABLE 3.2.
Prep Schools in the Social Elite

Andover (Andover, Mass.)
Asheville (Asheville, N.C.)
Buckley (New York City)
Cate (Carpinteria, Calif.)
Catlin Gabel (Portland, Ore.)
Choate (Wallingford, Conn.)
Cranbrook (Bloomfield Hills, Mich.)
Country Day School (St. Louis)
Deerfield (Deerfield, Mass.)
Episcopal High (Alexandria, Va.)
Exeter (Exeter, N.H.)
Gilman (Baltimore)
Groton (Groton, Mass.)
Hill (Pottstown, Pa.)
Hotchkiss (Lakeville, Conn.)
Kingswood (Hartford, Conn.)
Kent (Kent, Conn.)
Lake Forest (Lake Forest, Ill.)
Lakeside (Seattle)
Lawrenceville (Lawrenceville, N.J.)

Middlesex (Concord, Mass.)
Milton (Milton, Mass.)
Moses Brown (Providence)
Pomfret (Pomfret, Conn.)
Portsmouth Priory (Portsmouth, R.I.)
Punahou (Honolulu)
St. Andrew's (Middlebury, Del.)
St. Christopher's (Richmond)
St. George's (Newport, R.I.)
St. Mark's (Southborough, Mass.)
St. Paul's (Concord, N.H.)
Shattuck (Fairbault, Minn.)
Taft (Watertown, Conn.)
Thacher (Ojai, Calif.)
University School (Cleveland)
University School (Milwaukee)
Webb (Bell Buckle, Tenn.)
Westminister (Atlanta)
Woodberry Forest (Woodberry Forest, Va.)

that they attended elite prep schools with a higher frequency than the Jews, and that difference is so slight as to be meaningless (17.4 percent as oposed to 16.6 percent).

Our data on prep schools, limited though they may be, indicate that successful Jews in the corporate and philanthropic world are as likely or more likely to have attended elite prep schools as their non-Jewish counterparts. And as was true for those who were in primarily non-Jewish clubs, the Jewish prep school graduates were more likely to be of German than Eastern European background, and were very likely to go on to prestigious Ivy League colleges.

What do we know about the kinds of experiences that Jews have had in these schools? Though in many ways separated from the mainstream of society, private schools have not avoided the racism and anti-Semitism found in the culture at large. In fact, there is substantial evidence that racism and anti-Semitism have been very much a part of the snobbery that characterizes these schools. Even one of the century's most respected political liberals, Adlai Stevenson, who attended Choate and then Princeton, was not unaffected. Biographer John Martin, after depicting one of Stevenson's surprisingly frequent anti-Semitic remarks, explained:

> The remark about Jews just noted was not an isolated instance. It flawed Stevenson's attitudes for years. In considering it, one must remember that Stevenson was, like us all, a product of his time and his place. His place was the Midwest, plus Eastern schools attended largely by the sons of the wealthy, white, Protestant, and well-born; during those years and in those places and among those people, such utterances were simply made heedlessly (Martin, 1976: 71).

Paul Cowan, who attended Choate 40 years after Stevenson, describes the casualness and frequency of the racism there in the following way:

> At Choate, during the Eisenhower years, racist remarks were as much a part of our daily lives as the chapel services which we were required to attend each night. In fact, at the first Sunday service I attended there, Seymour St. John, the school's headmaster and also its chaplain, began his sermon with a joke about "Old Darky Joe" and his friend "Moe." The humor that the sons of America's (mostly Republican) elite shared with one another was considerably blunter (Cowan, 1967: 4)

Nor was Choate free from acts of anti-Semitism. Cowan also relates how he, one of the few Jewish students, had the words "FUCK YOU, YOU KIKE" written on his math book by one of his classmates.

Although some acknowledged the presence of anti-Semitism at their boarding schools, the Jewish corporate directors we spoke with who had attended such schools had much fonder memories of them than did Cowan. The few who indicated that the experience had been particularly difficult because they were Jewish were strong in their convictions that the benefits far outweighed the difficulties. Joseph F. Cullman, for example, described to us his experiences as a student at Hotchkiss in the late 1920s in the following way:

> There was quite a bit of anti-Semitism at that time. I was one of very few Jews there. At that time it was more of an elitist school than it is now, somewhat more catholic and eclectic. There were only three or four Jewish students, and most of the other students weren't accustomed to social encounters with Jews. To me, Hotchkiss was one of the most important moves I ever made in my life. I started out in a nice comfortable community happy as a clam. So when my father decided I should go to Hotchkiss—in those days we didn't ask the children the

way we do today, now you've got to go through new procedures, but in those days he said "You're going to Hotchkiss"—I did and I survived it. But it was a difficult emotional experience.

Cullman's loyalty to Hotchkiss is indicated by his service on its board for ten years, as well as by several large financial contributions. He is but one of a number of Jews on our lists who have joined the boards of the prep schools they attended.

Typically, we have found that the Jewish private school graduates in the corporate community have stayed in close touch with their school friends (in closer touch than with the friends they made in college). Ezra Zilkha, a graduate of The Hill School, told us that he was in much more frequent contact with his Hill School friends, who included Nelson Bunker Hunt, John Bunting, and the Stevenson brothers, than with his college friends. Similarly, when we asked John Weinberg if he stayed in contact with his Deerfield friends, he replied, "Always. I'm a trustee at Deerfield."

There are considerations other than prestige and a good education that go into deciding whether or not to send one's children to prep school. One of these is where one lives and the nature of the public schools there. In New York City there was no doubt on the part of the corporate directors we spoke with that their children would go off to a boarding school—the only real decision was where they would go. John Weinberg's son went to Deerfield, as he had, and his daughter went to Choate. Joseph Cullman had no sons, but his grandson went to Hotchkiss as he had half a century earlier. And Simon Rifkind, who came to America from Russia as a nine-year-old child, and said that when he went to public high school, "for the first time, I discovered America," sent his sons to Loomis. By then, of course, he had become a federal judge. As for his choice of Loomis, he said that he simply asked David Rockefeller where he had sent his children, and sent his sons to the same school.

Other directors, in other cities, were less likely to view private school as an automatic choice. In Chicago, for instance, many of the directors we spoke with live in comfortable bedroom communities on the north shore, where the public schools are known to be excellent. As a result, some of their children went to public schools. For example, Maynard Wishner, president of Walter Heller, did not hesitate to send his two daughters to the public schools in Evanston. Others, such as Inland Steel's Joseph and Phillip Block, attended private schools and sent their children to private schools. And some, like Jay Pritzker, did both: two of his five children attended New Trier High School, a public school, and three attended private day schools in the Chicago area (Jay Pritzker himself had gone to Francis Parker, a private day school on the north side of Chicago). Similarly, in Minneapolis, if parents decide to take their children out of the public schools, they are unlikely to send them East but rather to the Blake School in that same city. In Seattle, a few of the wealthier Jewish families send their children to the Lakeside School, but most attend public schools.

Although the question of whether or not to send one's children to private school may vary from city to city, those corporate directors we spoke with who had sent their children to public schools were decidedly in the minority. In fact, our interviews indicate that the children of corporate directors have been much more likely to attend prestigious prep schools than the corporate directors themselves. This, we believe, not only is evidence of the importance of such schools as routes to the upper class, but evidence for our contention that the clubs are not the only means of social interaction for corporate gentiles and Jews. Let us turn now to yet another opportunity for such interaction: the boards of directors of the cultural elite.

THE CULTURAL ELITE

The boards of major cultural institutions include names such as Astor, Auchincloss, and Rockefeller, names that are and have long been very much a part of the Protestant Establishment. Our interviews with Jewish members of the corporate elite convinced us that these cultural institutions provide yet another basis for social contact between Jewish and gentile members of the corporate elite.

There are many reasons for involving oneself in the activities of the cultural institutions of one's city. Richard Sherwood, the chairman of the board of the Los Angeles County Museum, told us that his wife, an art history major at Wellesley while he was majoring in political science at Yale, had encouraged him to read some of her art books while he was in the military during the Korean war. He did, and when they returned to live in their hometown of Los Angeles in 1955, they became active in volunteer work at one of the local museums. When we asked if the others on his board shared his long-time involvement in the arts, Sherwood responded in the following manner:

> Cultural organizations attract people for complex reasons. Some because they have a passion for the particular form of expression and therefore come forward. Others because they believe it's a matter of civic virtue, and you ought to have in a city like this a great symphony, or a great whatever. Others because it's a very comfortable ladder up into a set of worlds. I guess in any cultural institution there's a mixture

of aesthetes, parvenues and people who think it's just part of their establishment civic responsibility.

Sidney Brody, one of Sherwood's predecessors as chairman of the Los Angeles County Museum, and one of the three major fundraisers for that museum, told us how fundraising for the museum and the Music Center had helped create a sense of community in Los Angeles, and has led to increased cooperation between Jewish and gentile members of that city's corporate elite:

> The Jews have become much more active in a cross-section of the community, and I think one thing that furthered that was the building and creating of the Los Angeles County Museum and the Music Center. There were sizable sums of money raised in a short period of time— some $30 million, about $15 million each initially, and it's grown considerably since that. And in order to do that it penetrated the community. It not only broke down on a cooperative effort religious and ethnic differences, but contributed to a sense of "village identification." It pulled together into homogeneous Los Angeles what was Santa Monica, Pasadena, isolated pockets, because these were two major cultural activities which dominate the community. As a result, I think there has been much more social interchange as people have gotten to know each other much better through that type of community activity.

Brody suspects that there was a personal corporate reward for him as well, though that was not what motivated him to work as a fundraiser and a director for the museum. When we asked how he had come to be on the board of Security Pacific (the 11th largest bank in 1981), he told us: "I was asked to go on the board probably because of my involvement in the community as one of the three fundraisers who built the museum. I had a lot of community identification from doing that, at the time they were trying to identify people who had some visibility in the community and in civic activities."

Even some of the Jews in our study got to know each other through cultural boards. When we asked one director how he had met two prominent members of the New York Jewish community, he mentioned several civic involvements they shared in common, including the board of the Metropolitan Opera.

Cultural institutions, then, are yet another avenue of social contact for members of the corporate and social elites. In order to establish empirically that such contact does include Jews and gentiles, and to get some sense of the frequency with which it occurs, we investigated the boards of the most important cultural institutions in New York, Chicago, and Los Angeles. We obtained lists of the boards for the five major museums in New York (they are, alphabetically, the American Museum of Natural History, the Guggenheim, the Metropolitan Museum of Art, the Museum of Modern Art, and the Whitney), as well as for the Lincoln Center for the Performing Arts and for the Metropolitan Opera. For Chicago, we obtained lists of the boards of what one of our informants referred to as "the big three": the Art Institute, the Lyric Opera, and the Chicago Symphony Orchestra. And for Los Angeles we looked at the boards of what generally seemed to be considered "the two premier cultural institutions," the Los Angeles County Museum and the Music Center (an umbrella institution that includes a variety of cultural institutions in Los Angeles, such as the opera, the philharmonic, and the Hollywood Bowl). We looked up the names of the 504 board members who sat on one or more of these cultural institutions in *Who's Who in America*, *Trustees of Wealth*, and our most recent membership lists for the Harmonie Club, the Standard Club, and the Hillcrest Country Club.

There can be no doubt that the cultural elite is drawn from the very same corporate and social circles Baltzell wrote about in *The Protestant Establishment* and we have been writing about in this book. Aside from the obviously familiar names of Rockefeller, Auchincloss, and Astor, there were many men with many directorships on major corporate boards on our list of trustees. A clear majority of those we were able to find in our biographical sources were members of at least one of the clubs on our list, and many belonged to more than one of these clubs. Their biographies were strewn with references to their having attended and been trustees of the most prestigious prep schools in the country. And we were not surprised to find that of those 64 who chose to indicate their religion in their biographical sketches, 33 were Episcopalians and 12 were Presbyterians. (If one were to have bet on the apparently unchanging figure of 85 percent that various studies have found to represent the frequency of Protestants in the corporate elite, one would have overestimated, but only slightly—in this case, 83 percent were Protestant, and 85 percent of these were either Episcopalians or Presbyterians.)

Nestled among the names of the members of the Protestant Establishment were 61 people we were able to identify as Jewish. These 61 people constitute 12.1 percent of all the trustees of the 12 cultural institutions. Separate analyses for the three cities indicated that our findings were remarkably similar in the three cities: We were able to identify 12.3 percent of the New York board members as Jewish, 12.3 percent of the Chicago board members, and 11.2 percent of the Los Angeles board members. Clearly there are Jewish members of what is a predominantly gentile cultural elite and, as a result, there is yet another avenue for social interaction along with the clubs and the prep schools. Laurence Tisch, who went to a public high school and has no interest in joining the Links or any of the other elite WASP clubs, is on the board of the Whitney—as is Mrs. Laurence Rockefeller. Walter Annenberg and Arthur O. Sulzberger are not in the same clubs as Arthur Houghton, Jr. (of the Corning Glass Works Houghtons, and a director of U.S. Steel, among others) and J. Richardson Dilworth (Chase Manhattan Bank, among others), but they do sit on the board of the Metropolitan Museum with them.

This is not to say that Tisch, Annenberg, or Sulzberger—or the other Jewish trustees on the boards of the other cultural institutions we have looked at—benefit economically from their social contact with members of the Protestant Establishment. It is, however, an assertion that the clubs are not the only game in town when it comes to social contact between upper-class gentiles and upper-class Jews. We do not assume that the members of these boards discuss their own business interests with one another at their meetings, or at the gala openings of major exhibits or performances (though they may). We do assume, as Jay Pritzker suggested in his comments about clubs, that relationships that originate in a social context may ultimately prove to be useful in other ways.

CONCLUSION

Our look at three components of the social elite—clubs, prep schools, and the boards of major cultural institutions—indicates that Jewish corporate leaders do have social contact with gentile members of the corporate elite. Not many Jews are members of the most prestigious WASP clubs. Most of those we have been able to identify who are members of these clubs are from old-line German-Jewish families; the few who are not are, like the German Jews, from families that have had money for some time. The more recently successful Eastern European Jews expressed little interest in joining WASP clubs, though they are likely to be members of Jewish clubs like the Harmonie or the Standard. In contrast to the club world, we have found that Jewish corporate leaders are as likely as their non-Jewish counterparts to have attended elite prep schools, and the friendships formed during these years with other wealthy Jewish and gentile children seem to be lasting ones. And, as with the prep schools, we have found that Jews are very much a part of the cultural elite. We do not assume that we have exhausted the avenues of potential social interaction. A number of the directors we interviewed also mentioned hospital boards, university boards, and various fundraising activities, such as the United Way, as means of getting to know members of the gentile elite.

Therefore, we conclude that the restrictive policies of elite clubs have not prevented Jews from becoming successful corporate leaders (though, for some, it may have altered the path that they took), and these policies have not prevented successful corporate leaders who are also Jewish from interacting socially with the predominantly Protestant Establishment. Because of the prep schools, the cultural institutions, and other sources of social contact that we have not considered in any depth in this chapter, it is our belief that Jews in the corporate elite do not need the clubs to meet the club members—they are likely to know them from their days in school together, or from other social contexts. It is in this sense that Ezra Zilkha was correct when he claimed that "clubs have become irrelevant." And these numerous sources of social contact also explain why so many of the men we interviewed told us that they were frequently *guests* in the elite WASP clubs. Simon Rifkind, a Russian immigrant with no interest in joining a WASP club, mentioned that he had eaten dinner at the Links the night before. John Weinberg's response to our question about these clubs was, "I've been in them all, I go there all the time, I know a lot of people there, but never had any interest in becoming a member." We can only conclude that the club barrier is surely an anachronism, as Baltzell argued two decades ago, but it is a much less significant one than he thought.

Chapter 4

Southern Jews in The Corporate and Social Elites

JEWS IN THE SOUTH

Because most members, and especially most Jewish members, of the national corporate and social elites live in major urban centers, so far in this book we have focused primarily on residents of cities such as New York, Boston, Chicago, Los Angeles, and San Francisco. In this chapter we will shift that focus to another region of the country (the South) and to two cities within that region (Greensboro and Winston-Salem, North Carolina).

Aside from the need to consider the experiences of Jews in local elites outside the major cities, we believe that the South is of particular interest for a number of reasons. One of these is that the South was once home for many American Jews, and it was the stepping stone for many of the great American Jewish fortunes. Because of the economic opportunities, as well as the political and religious freedoms specified in the charters of some of the southern colonies, many Sephardic and early German Jews who came to America settled in the South. It is established that in 1770 fully 25 percent of the Jews in America lived in the South (Lavender, 1977: 9). In 1800, two of the four largest Jewish communities were in southern cities: Charleston, South Carolina was the largest, with 500 families; New York was the second largest, with about 400 families; Philadelphia was the third; and Richmond, Virginia was fourth with slightly over 30 households (Berman, 1979: 29–30 and Reznikoff, 1950: 67).

In addition, when the second major wave of Jewish immigration to this country occurred, many came to the South to earn a living (though by this time a much smaller percentage of the American Jewish population lived in the South). Supple's (1957) detailed account of the origins of

New York's German-Jewish investment bankers reveals that members of a number of these families started out as peddlers in the South. Henry Lehman, after arriving from Bavaria in 1844, was a peddler in Alabama for a year, and then opened a store in Montgomery. Samuel Rosenwald (the father of the future president of Sears, Roebuck) also peddled in the South until the Civil War broke out, at which time he moved north to Springfield, Illinois. James Seligman, one of the eight Seligman brothers to arrive from Bavaria between 1837 and 1843, went to Alabama as a peddler. He was so successful that in 1841 three more Seligman brothers accompanied him to Alabama and, by 1843, they were operating four stores there. Supple (1957: 154) concludes:

> Thus, by the late 1850s the initial phase of economic integration was largely completed. Twenty years had witnessed the arrival of a genera-tion of German Jews with little capital. Among them were men who, seeing their opportunity in the field of distribution, launched forth inland yet more hundreds of miles. Some stayed out in the West and the South and their children established permanent communities, but another cluster also emerged: men who, back in New York with capital and commercial experience, would ultimately participate to no small extent in the critical development of the American capital market in the decades after the Civil War.

As Supple states, many German Jews who came to the South stayed. During the 1850s the number of Jewish synagogues in the South grew from 6 to 17. By the start of the Civil War, there were sizable Jewish communities in Louisville, Kentucky; Wilmington, North Carolina; Augusta, Columbus and Macon, Georgia; Mobile and Montgomery, Alabama; New Orleans, Louisiana; and, of course, in Charleston, South Carolina, and Richmond, Virginia (Dinnerstein and Palsson, 1973: 27).

In 1850, when Isaac Mayer Wise, who was to become the leader of Reform Judaism in the United States, visited Charleston to consider a position as "hazan" (literally "reader," a position that corresponded to rabbi in the Sephardic congregation), he was impressed with the status, sophistication, and acceptance of the Jewish community there. Wise later wrote that he was "much taken with Charleston," that he was "domiciled in splendid rooms," that a Negro was at his "disposal," that the city and its inhabitants were "so refined and cultured," and that, for the first time in his life, he was "the guest of American aristocrats." He did not, how-ever, take the job, staying in Albany due to the urgings of his friends there and his wife's concern with the incidence of yellow fever in Charles-ton (Reznikoff, 1950: 147).

Another reason that the South is of particular interest to our investigation of Jews in the Protestant Establishment is suggested by Wise's description of Charleston in 1850: the presence or absence of anti-Semitism. Despite the findings of various researchers that Southerners score higher than residents of other regions on various paper and pencil measures of anti-Semitism (see, for example, Adorno et al., 1950; Glock and Stark, 1966; Selznick and Steinberg, 1969) many who grew up in the South, and some who did not, have claimed that it is the region in America that has been the least anti-Semitic. Harry Golden, the journalist whose books *Only in America* (1944) and *For 2¢ Plain* (1943) were best sellers, has been the most vociferous in his defense of the South. He has argued that the South not only has been the nicest place for Jews to live in America, but that it "has provided the most favorable 'atmosphere' the Jewish people have known in the modern world" (Golden, 1955; 6, 11).

Golden's assertions have been echoed by Eli Evans (1974), another Jewish southerner who wrote a book titled *The Provincials: A Personal History of Jews in the South*. Evans, now a New York lawyer and foundation executive, grew up in Durham, North Carolina, where his father was the first Jew to be elected mayor. He writes: "I don't think that most Jews in the South would agree with the findings of the polls and the studies, for most Jews live their lives in a placid atmosphere as part of the white majority" (1974: 226).

John Higham (1975: 164), a historian, believes that the fact that Jews in the South have been able to be part of the white majority is the very reason they have experienced so little discrimination. His argument might be termed the "lightning rod" theory: because blacks received the brunt of outgroup prejudice, Jews, being white, were treated as part of the dominant majority. He points out that the two areas that have been celebrated for not discriminating against Jews—the South and San Francisco—both had this "lightning rod" variable in common:

If we examine the areas of low discrimination, two circumstances stand out. Both the South and San Francisco fought for decades to uphold white supremacy in the face of a colored race, the Negro in one, the Oriental in the other. For a long time this overriding preoccupation bound all white men together as partners and equals. By the time other ethnic issues intruded, the Jews had become more fully integrated in the local culture than anywhere else. As late as 1916, the leading anti-Japanese organization in San Francisco, the Native Sons of the Golden West, held a mass meeting to raise funds for persecuted European Jews. The Grand President of the Native Sons, forgetting for the moment the Oriental issue, asked San Francisco to "say to all mankind that there exists in this world one spot at least where every citizen is within the pale."

If the view of the South put forth by writers such as Golden, Evans, and Higham is correct, then it becomes a particularly important region to look at in our attempt to understand the interaction between Jews and the Protestant Establishment. If indeed there has been a minimal amount of anti-Semitism in the South, and among the southern elite, then we would expect to find that Jews have been accepted into local southern elites to a considerable degree. If, on the other hand, the high level of southern anti-Semitism found on paper and pencil tests accurately characterizes the region and its local elites, we would expect to find an absence of Jews in upper-class institutions in the South.

The historical record depicting Southern Jewry is piecemeal, and is based especially on accounts of those cities such as Charleston and Richmond that have had sizable Jewish communities for a considerable length of time. As Dinnerstein and Palsson (1973: 389) put it in their book on *Jews in the South*, "the literature on southern Jews is thin." Furthermore, those accounts that do exist rarely focus on the issue of interest here, namely, the interactions between upper-class Jews and gentiles. When they do, they usually provide anecdotal rather than empirical evidence.

However, there has been a noteworthy increase in academic interest in Southern Jewry since World War II. A number of scholars have turned their attention to the experiences of the Jewish communities in various Southern cities. Two such cities are Atlanta and New Orleans. In the late 1940s, Solomon Sutker studied the Atlanta Jewish community. Sutker (1958: 262) wrote the following about the Jewish social clubs of Atlanta: "A major reason for the existence of these Jewish social clubs lies in the fact that the Jewish population is excluded from the other major social clubs of that city." The controversy that surrounded the revelation that two of Jimmy Carter's appointees, Griffin Bell and Bert Lance, were members of the exclusive and restricted Piedmont Driving Club indicates that in the ensuing 25 years things had not changed on this score.

Similarly, Leonard Reissman (1973: 291) reported that there is an upper-class Jewish community in New Orleans, based on "wealth, position and the length of time one's family has lived in New Orleans," but that it has not become a part of the most elite social circles. He stressed the "Catholic character of the city," and the importance of the social exclusivity surrounding the annual Mardi Gras celebration:

> There is no question that some Jews belong to Mardi Gras krewes, although there is ground to question whether they belong to those with highest status. ... Some families, it is said, leave the city during Mardi Gras, perhaps to avoid what may seem to them an unpleasant confrontation.
>
> The same kind of barrier or ceiling also exists for membership in the elite clubs, which intermesh with the status structure of the krewes.

> One of the two highest ranking clubs, it has been said, has claimed that no Jew has ever got beyond the foyer in the building it occupies. Whether apocryphal or true, the statement is indicative of a generally accepted point of view (1973: 302).

Reissman pointed out that the upper-class Jewish community has reacted to these slights by using similar criteria to establish its own exclusiveness. He mentions its considerable emphasis on genealogy as well as wealth and position, and concluded: "I have no definite information on this point, but it is my impression that entry into the Jewish elite is as jealously controlled as that into any elite" (1973: 292).

More recently, Petrusak and Steinert (1976: 341) conducted a study of the Jewish community in Charleston. Though most of their findings are not relevant in this particular context, one is: 83 percent of their Jewish respondents disagreed with the statement that "Jews are accepted in social circles." However, there is no indication of whether or not the responses of upper-class Jews to this item differed from those of other Jews.

While these few studies are by no means definitive, they do not suggest a picture of Jewish acceptance that is greater than most Northern cities. To consider the question more closely, let us turn to our research on two southern cities, Greensboro and Winston-Salem, North Carolina (Zweigenhaft, 1978, 1979). These two cities provide us with an interesting comparison. They are remarkably similar in size (both encompass 60.6 square miles), and population (both between 140,000 and 160,000 as of the late 1970s), each has two Jewish congregations (one reform, one conservative) and they are close enough to each other to share the same airport. Yet, as we shall see, the degree to which Jews have been accepted into the local elites in these two cities has differed markedly.

GREENSBORO, NORTH CAROLINA

The Cones

One of the many young Jews to leave Bavaria in the middle of the nineteenth century was a 17-year-old named Herman Kahn. Just as his fellow Bavarian immigrants Marcus Goldman, Henry Lehman, Joseph Seligman, and Levi Strauss were to lay the groundwork for great family fortunes, so did Herman Kahn. The early years were not easy for him. Although he did all he could to become "American" as quickly as possible—including changing his last name from "Kahn" to "Cone"—his language difficulties and "Old World" appearance apparently made him somewhat of an embarrassment to his sister, Elise, who had been living in Richmond for some years. According to the family history, she and other members of the family "wanted him out of town badly enough to furnish a stock of goods and a horse and wagon from which to peddle in the country" (Cone, S., Unpublished: 27).

Not long thereafter, Herman Cone settled in Lunenberg County, Virginia, between Richmond and Danville. Another sister, Sophie, had come to America to marry a recent immigrant named Jacob Adler, and Herman and Jacob opened a small store together. A while later they tried moving their store to Richmond, but they did not do well and soon found themselves looking for another location.

In 1853, Herman and Jacob headed west from Roanoke in a "carry all," a covered wagon on springs, with no specific destination in mind. They drove more than 200 miles, came to Jonesboro, Tennessee, liked it, and settled in. They opened another store there, and alternated peddling and minding the store on a weekly basis.

By 1863 they had done well enough economically, and had become Southern enough in their attitudes, to invest $4,500 for "the purchase of three Negro slaves 'named Joe, William and Friendly.'" They lost their investment, however, when the Union won the Civil War (Korn, 1973: 106).

In 1870—by that time, married and the father of seven children—Herman Cone moved his family to Baltimore, where he established a successful grocery business. His sons, Moses and Ceasar, gradually took over the business and in 1890, they organized the Cone Export and Commission Company, financed largely by the grocery business. It was a selling and finance agent for southern cotton mills. As Moses traveled to stores throughout the Piedmont of North Carolina, he also developed an understanding of the ways the mills were run and, especially, of their business shortcomings. He found that many of these small independent mills had the same problem: not enough capital to buy cotton when needed. In fact, many of the mill villages paid the Cones for their groceries with yarn or cloth.

So Moses made an offer: He would provide cash to the mills if they would give him a monopoly on their goods. Such monopolies were not illegal, and many mill owners were delighted with this arrangement by which they would do the producing and the Cones would do the selling. Within a year, Cone Export and Commission Company, with offices in New York City, was selling for 47 different cotton mills throughout North Carolina, and the Cone brothers were on their way to a huge fortune. However, as successful as they were in selling for the mills, the real fortune developed as the Cones began to purchase the mills.

In 1895, a mill owned by the Cones in Greensboro, the Proximity

Mill, began production. This mill did so well that Greensboro became the main headquarters for the company which, by 1904, had more than a million dollars in common stock. The Cone family maintained, as it does today, majority interest. When Moses died in 1908, his personal fortune was sizable enough for him to leave behind a 35,000 acre estate in the North Carolina mountains with such a large house on it that, as the *Greensboro Daily News* asserted, "it would be called a mansion in New York or a castle in the old country." His will also provided for a hospital that was to be built in Greensboro, the Moses H. Cone Hospital.

Thus it was that Herman Kahn became Cone and his two oldest sons guided the family business into textiles in Greensboro. Cone Mills became the world's leading producer of denim, corduroy, and flannel. The family fortune was so large that steady incomes were provided for sisters Etta and Claribel in Baltimore who traveled widely and became celebrated for their friendship with Gertrude Stein. They also inadvertently made additional millions by purchasing numerous pieces from several struggling artist friends of Gertrude Stein's, including Picasso and Matisse (Cone, E. T., 1973; Mellow, 1974: 92; Pollack, 1962: 78).

The impact of the Cone family and its company on the city of Greensboro has been massive. In 1920, when the population was a mere 20,000, Cone Mills employed approximately 3,000 people. The Cone family grew, participated in various forms of leadership in the community and—as we shall see—assimilated into the local upper class. This included acceptance by such local bastions of the upper crust as the Greensboro Country Club, and it included a good bit of marrying out of the faith. Though the population of Greensboro is much larger today than 60 years ago, and the percentage of residents employed by Cone Mills much smaller than in 1920, the family's impact is still quite visible: schools, the hospital, and roads are named after various Cones. Thus for the past 75 years the Jews of Greensboro have lived in a town where among the most prominent, wealthy, and visible people has been a Jewish family named Cone. It is in this context that we turn to a consideration of the degree to which the Jewish community of Greensboro has been accepted into the higher circles and general community life of that city.

The Present Study

We looked at various indices of local economic power and social prestige in order to identify the extent to which Greensboro Jews have become part of the local power structure. Essentially what we did was (1) obtain membership lists for the temple, the synagogue, the local country clubs and an exclusive downtown dining club; (2) look up membership on boards of directors of Greensboro-based companies that were listed in

Dun & Bradstreet's *Million Dollar Directory* (1976); and (3) cross-check the lists to look for overlap.

In addition, we interviewed Jewish residents of Greensboro. These interviews, conducted over a period of months, were not a random sample of the Jews in Greensboro. Rather, we started with individuals whom we could identify, on the basis of the overlap analysis, as key figures. We then used what is called a "snowball approach" to expand outward into the Jewish community, interviewing those people suggested to us in the first set of interviews. By the time we had finished, we had spoken with people of varying ages, social classes, and lengths of residence in Greensboro.

We found, first of all, that all four of the most prestigious social clubs in Greensboro have Jewish members. The Greensboro Country Club, which at the time had 943 members, included 24 people who were members of one of the two Jewish congregations (2.5 percent). Sedgefield Country Club, with a membership of 426 and located midway between the cities of Greensboro and High Point, included eight people who were members of one of Greensboro's two Jewish congregations (1.5 percent). And the Greensboro City Club, a downtown dining club, included in its 681-person membership 41 people who were members of one of the two Jewish congregations (6.0 percent). The fourth club, Starmount Country Club, is considered by many as "the Jewish country club," but Starmount does not have a membership booklet for its members, and its leadership would not provide us with a membership roster. We therefore had to rely on estimates, by members of Starmount, of the percentage of members at Starmount that is Jewish. Their estimates ranged from as low as 15 percent to as high as 70 percent.

There were several striking qualities in the findings. First, for the three clubs for which we had membership lists, the Jewish club members were much more likely to be members of the reform temple rather than of the conservative synagogue. Approximately 90 percent of the Jewish club members were affiliated with the temple, and only 10 percent with the synagogue. This is in general agreement with findings elsewhere that reform congregations are more likely to include wealthier members and those of German-Jewish extraction than are conservative congregations (Waxman, 1981: 82).

A second noteworthy characteristic of our results is that the percentage of Jewish members in these clubs is, in the case of one club, equal to, and in the case of the other three, greater than the percentage of Jews in the Greensboro population. Though the percentage of Jews in North Carolina is generally estimated to be a mere 0.2 percent (Fine and Himmelfarb, 1978: 257; Sloan, 1978: 18), there is certainly a higher proportion of Jews in Greensboro than in the state at large. Our estimate, based on the number of families in the two congregations and recent census data on average family size, suggests that 1.5 percent of the Greensboro population is Jewish by our criteria.

We also looked at the extent to which the members of the Jewish community are involved in the economic elite of their city. To determine this, we looked up the names of the directors of the Greensboro based companies listed in Dun & Bradstreet's *Million Dollar Directory*, and cross-checked them with the synagogue and temple membership lists. There were 63 Greensboro companies listed in the directory, including 6 companies that made the *Fortune* list in 1976: Burlington Industries (#104); Blue Bell (#301); Cone Mills (#367); Texfi Industries (#662); Guilford Mills (#952); and Jefferson Pilot (the 33rd largest life insurance company that year). We found that 14 of the 417 directors (or 3.4 percent) were Jewish. Again this figure exceeds our estimate of the percentage of Jews in the Greensboro population, and again the individuals were mostly members of the reform temple rather than the conservative synagogue (11 of the 14 were members of the temple).

A closer look at the 14 Jewish directors reveals that 10 of them are drawn from three families. In addition to the four Cones who sat on the board of Cone Mills, three were from the Bates family (of Bates Nite-wear), and three were from the Davidson family (of Davidson Supply). The other four were Martin Bernstein and Lawrence Cohen (both of The Jewel Box of Greensboro), Maurice Fishman (of Guilford Mills), and Sidney Stern, Jr. (of United Guaranty). No members of the Greensboro Jewish community were on the boards of the three largest Greensboro based corporations (Burlington Industries, Blue Bell, and Jefferson Pilot Corporation). Indeed, other than the Cones' directorships on Cone Mills, and Fishman's directorship on the board of Guilford Mills (another textile company), there were no Greensboro Jews on the boards of other *Fortune*-level corporations or on other boards in Greensboro's top ten corporations. It appears that despite the enormous influence of the Cones, and the obvious social acceptance of Jews into the upper-class clubs of the community, the presence of Jews in the local corporate elite has continued to consist of involvement in corporations started by Jews. This is consistent with what we found at the national level.

These findings provide additional evidence that calls into question Baltzell's assumptions about the relationship between clubs and corporations. In the case of Greensboro, Jews are in the social clubs, but they have not been taken on the boards of companies they did not start. Once again, the club tail did not wag the corporate dog.

Concerns About Anti-Semitism

For the most part, our interviews with members of the Greensboro Jewish community confirmed the predominantly rosy picture suggested by the data we have just described. The people we spoke with like living in Greensboro, have experienced very little anti-Semitism, and are proud of the way Jews have been accepted into the broader community.

Yet, despite their near unanimity in proclaiming a minimum of anti-Semitism in Greensboro, the Jews we interviewed were quite aware of the possibility of being excluded in certain ways as a result of being Jewish. Two Jewish members of the Greensboro Country Club separately referred to their current concerns that there may be a quota—that has been reached—for Jews at "the country club." The pervasive and deep-rooted concern that anti-Semitism could surface, even in as comfortable an environment as Greensboro, was expressed by a man who might be expected to be least likely to worry. Ben Cone, Sr., the oldest Cone of his generation (77 at the time of the interview), former mayor of the city (1949–1951), member of the Greensboro Country Club and the Greensboro City Club, a former member of the board of directors at Cone Mills, and married to a non-Jew, told us that although he was "never particularly aware of any, there's always latent anti-Semitism, still is."

Some people pointed out that despite the widespread acceptance of Jews in the clubs, and their obvious involvement in the city's cultural, economic and political life, they had been almost completely frozen out of one upper-class social arena—the debutante scene and the Junior League. Over the years, only a handful of young Jewish women had been invited to "come out," which, according to one woman we spoke with, had "devastated" one or two of them. When we checked the debutante lists in the local paper over a four-year period in the mid-1970s, this pattern was confirmed. We were able to find only one Jewish debutante out of the 113 participating in this rite of passage (see Bossard and Boll, 1948). Along the same lines, there was a notable dearth of Jewish women in the Greensboro chapter of the Junior League. This is not so surprising when one considers that "League members are also, to a large extent, debutantes and former debutantes" (Birmingham, 1958: 122–123). There were 336 "active" members of the Junior League in 1976, and another 378 "sustaining" members (which means they were over 40, for the most part inactive, but still paid yearly dues). Of these 714 women, four were Jewish (0.6 percent); all four were sustaining members, and two were members of the Cone family. Ironically, one of these women had served a term as president of the organization, and it was her daughter who was the sole Jewish debutante from 1973 to 1976.

Assimilation at the Top

In spite of the almost total absence of Jews among debutantes and in the Junior League, there has been nonetheless a notable pattern of assimilation by the wealthiest Jews in the community. This was most clearly apparent in the marriage patterns within the Cone family. Moses Cone married a Jewish woman, but they had no children. Ceasar Cone, the second son, married Jeannette Siegel of New York's "our crowd," and they had three sons—Herman, Benjamin, and Ceasar II. Ceasar's oldest son, Herman, married a Jewish woman, Louise Wolf, but both Benjamin and Ceasar II married gentiles. Though some of the oldest people we interviewed indicated that the Jewish community was shocked back in 1937 when Benjamin Cone married Anne Wortham, an Episcopalian, he did not see it that way: "I don't think there was a negative or positive reaction. Happens every day. Arnold Schiffman did it too, several others had. My mother didn't exactly like it, but she came to be fond of my wife." A year and a half later, the third son, Ceasar II, married Martha Abercrombie, also an Episcopalian. These three Cones—Herman, Benjamin, and Ceasar II—had eight children and, as of the late 1970s, 17 grandchildren. Of the 17 grandchildren, three were being raised as Jews.

There have been some signs of reversal in the trend toward further assimilation in the Cone family, at least in one branch of it. Although Benjamin Cone's children were not raised as Jews, two have converted to Judaism, for different reasons. Benjamin, Jr., just had returned from Vietnam in 1967, and was greatly affected by the six-day war in Israel. He converted, and went on to head the Israeli bond campaign. He has remained active in Jewish community affairs, although, as he puts it, "I'm still a twice a year Jew—Rosh Hashonah and Yom Kippur." His wife is not Jewish and has no plans to convert; the children are being raised as Episcopalians. In 1974, his older sister, Jeannette, married a Jewish man and converted to Judaism. Nonetheless, there are now more non-Jewish Cones than Jewish Cones in Greensboro, a pattern that has been found for wealthy German Jews such as the Guggenheims in the north (Davis, 1979).

In addition to the high percentage of non-Jews among the Greensboro Cones, our interviews revealed that some of the wealthier members of the Jewish community had gone out of their way to demonstrate their distaste for their Jewish heritage. Evans (1974: 191) was surely correct in his claim that "the process of assimilation is subtle and goes beyond over-looking religious laws or marrying gentiles." But what has been striking about some of the wealthier Jews in Greensboro is not the subtlety of their assimilation, but the lack of it. The words and actions of some have offended the Jewish community, not simply in their acceptance of gentile attitudes (though that is part of it), but in the intensity and vehemence with which they have rejected their Jewish heritage. Two examples, not meant to be typical of Greensboro's wealthier Jews, illustrate the degree of "assimilation" to which some of the wealthier have gone.

The first concerns a man who came to Greensboro from a wealthy New Orleans family. He married into an even wealthier Greensboro family, and developed an immense amount of land, which is now worth many millions. His major development includes a country club, a large shopping center, and one of the most desirable neighborhoods in Greensboro. His children all married out of the faith, with most becoming Unitarians. He dropped his membership in Temple Emanuel and became a Unitarian.

For reasons that remain unclear, he decided that not only did he not want to be buried in the family plot at the Hebrew Cemetary, alongside his in-laws, but he also moved the remains of his in-laws to a non-Jewish cemetary. This enraged many members of the Jewish community. As one woman said when telling us this story (many told it to us), "It makes my blood boil to talk about it!"

The second example concerns a prominant member of the Jewish community. When we asked him about anti-Semitism in Greensboro, he replied:

> I'm anti-Semitic. I don't like Jews. I've been to meetings where they repulse me. Jews are more prejudiced than non-Jews. They're more against each other (as I am) and against letting non-Jews participate in what they're doing.

He went on to say:

> The anti-Semitism has grown in proportion to the number of northeast Jews who come down here to live. They've built up a certain amount of feeling that didn't exist before.... I hate to see the way they go about their business here. Take the Eastern Music Festival for example, it's become a Hebrew monopoly. I can't stand those festivals anymore because of the Jews.

In addition to the overtly anti-Semitic language, there is a striking parallel to the attitudes of many established German Jews around the turn of the century toward the incoming Eastern European Jews. Baltzell writes (1964: 302–303):

> Thus, the term "kike," first coined by German Jews as a derogatory stereotype applying to the new Russian immigrants, was now used by gentiles when referring to Jews in general, the cultivated and Americanized German as well as the impoverished and alien garment workers on the Lower East Side. This was, of course, a terrible shock to the established Jews, especially the cultivated elite, some of whom became anti-

Semitic themselves. For the outraged German Jew saw, shuffling down the gangplank, himself or his father, stripped of the accessories of respectability.

The Rabbi and His Wife

The more people we spoke with, the more apparent it became that one particular rabbi had played an unusually important role as a liaison between the Jewish community and the upper class gentile community. And, interestingly, so had his wife.

Rabbi Frederick Rypens came to Greensboro in 1931 to be the rabbi at Temple Emanuel. He remained in that position until he retired in 1959. Even his detractors, who did not feel he was traditional enough in his approach to Judaism, admit that he was a valuable link to the gentile community, and that he was "well liked" and "highly respected" in the broader community. He lived in the most exclusive neighborhood in Greensboro and was a member of the Greensboro Country Club (he had been given an honorary membership).

One of the first things mentioned about Rabbi Rypens was his appearance—that he was tall, silver haired, beautiful, and "not at all Jewish looking." One particular description, by a wealthy Jewish woman, was especially revealing: "Mr. Rypens was very handsome—a beautiful man. I used to think when he stood on the pulpit under the everlasting light, I used to think, that's maybe people's image of Jesus."

Rabbi Rypens had an extremely reformist attitude toward many Jewish beliefs. One woman told us: "[He] didn't even think bar mitzvah was necessary. He thought it was a totally wasted ceremony. They're not old enough to make any promises." Other examples could be given of the rabbi's preference for less traditional forms of Judaism. Suffice it to say that he was, as one person close to him put it, "reform reform."

Ruth Rypens, the rabbi's wife, also played a meaningful role in bringing the two communities together by creating an unusual one-year school in her home in the 1930s. For six years she tutored just one or two students full-time, but during the 1940s her classes increased in size to as large as 11 students. By the late 1940s, the school had become a pre-prep school: Mrs. Rypens taught the child for just one year, the ninth grade, and then the child went off to regular boarding school. By the late 1950s the word was that "she could get you in anywhere" when it came to elite prep schools. The school continued until 1970, spanning a period of 38 years.

During those 38 years, the rabbi's wife came into contact with the children of Greensboro's wealthiest families, Jewish and gentile alike. A look at the various class rosters reveals such locally prominent names as Preyer, Bowles, Bryan, Tannenbaum, Schiffman, and, of course, Cone. Of the 129 students who enrolled over the years at "Mrs. Rypens School" (as it was called), only 19 were Jewish. It was in this predominantly gentile atmosphere that Mrs. Rypens helped prepare these few Jewish students, academically and socially, for their entry into elite prep schools.

Before we conclude that Greensboro is typical of the South in the way Jews have been treated, let us turn to the nearby city of Winston-Salem which, as we will see, has had a very different history and has provided a very different kind of experience for its Jewish residents.

WINSTON-SALEM, NORTH CAROLINA

There was no Jewish family in Winston-Salem history whose economic success compared with that of the Cones in nearby Greensboro. Although there were a number of prosperous Jews in Winston-Salem, the most prominent families in economic terms were the Reynolds (of R. J. Reynolds Industries, the biggest company headquartered in the South) and the Hanes (of Hanes Underwear). This, we believe, is the single most important, though not the only, reason that the experience of Jews in Winston-Salem has been very different from that of Jews in Greensboro.

We performed our study of Winston-Salem in the same way that we had studied Greensboro, but our findings were strikingly different. There were no Jewish members of the two most prestigious country clubs, Olde Towne and Forsyth, nor did the Twin Cities Club, the exclusive downtown dining club, have Jewish members. Similarly, the corporate boards were virtually devoid of Jewish members. There were 59 corporations from Winston-Salem listed in the *Million Dollar Directory*, including five on the 1976 *Fortune* list: R. J. Reynolds (#48); Hanes Underwear (#482); Wachovia Corporation (the 36th largest bank that year); McLean Trucking and Piedmont Aviation (the 33rd and 47th largest transportation companies that year). Of the 386 people who sat on the boards of million dollar companies in Winston-Salem, only 4 were Jewish. Three of the four were brothers in a relatively small family business (Brenner Industries, the 11th largest in Winston-Salem that year) and the fourth, Max H. Crohn, Jr., a lawyer, sat on the board as general counsel of R. J. Reynolds Tobacco, a subsidiary of R. J. Reynolds Industries (he was not on the parent board, and has now left R. J. Reynolds to go into private practice). None was on the boards of the *Fortune*-level corporations.

Given these findings, we were not surprised to find that there were no Jewish women in the Winston-Salem Junior League. Members of the Jewish community in Winston-Salem were not surprised either, but they

of Greensboro's Cones have been raised as Jews, and that so many
been raised as Episcopalians, suggests special pressures to assimi-
t the top of the class structure. South or North, whether Cones
eensboro or Schiffs in New York, we find that those prominent
who become part of the economic and social elites are less and
lentifiable as Jews.

his finding brings us squarely up against the complex question of
elative importance of class identity and Jewish identity for the
ssful businessmen and their families who become part of the cor-
e and social elites. It is time to see if we can determine whether or
ass does overshadow ethnicity at the top of the status ladder.

were not happy about it. One woman we spoke with who had spent all
her life in Winston-Salem, and who has many childhood friends who are
now in the Junior League, told us that "It really does upset me." And
Morris Brenner (of Brenner Industries) expressed his feelings in the
following way: "For the most part I don't think the men give a damn about
the social exclusion. But it hurt me when my daughters weren't invited
to join the Junior League. When you or your children get a slap in the face,
it hurts."

In the early 1970s, the long-time absence of Jewish members from
the League was temporarily ended by the acceptance of two Jewish
women. One, Wendy Block, had transferred her membership when she
moved to Winston-Salem from Wilmington, but she only stayed a few
years and then moved back to Wilmington. The other, Vickie Ladmer
Bagley, was the daughter of an independent oil producer in Denver, and,
more important to the Winston-Salem Junior League, the second wife of
Smith Bagley, the grandson and heir of R. J. Reynolds. She was finally
admitted after having been voted down twice, but the Bagleys moved to
Washington, D.C. not long thereafter. The Winston-Salem Junior League
once again had no Jewish members.

The Jews of Winston-Salem with whom we spoke felt, for the most
part, that Winston-Salem was a decent city and had been a desirable
place in which to grow up. Most had not experienced a great deal of overt
anti-Semitism, but they had not felt especially accepted. As one prominent member of the Jewish community put it: "People here are comfortable with their own form of Christianity. The role of the Jews is very
peripheral—they just don't think about the Jews very much. Generally
speaking, they think neither positively nor negatively about Jews."

Of course, some Winston-Salem residents have thought negatively
enough of Jews to keep them out of the most prestigious private clubs,
and this fact rankles the Jewish community. One of the more prominent
Jewish businessmen told us that he had been encouraged by his friends
to apply for membership to the Forsyth Country Club and to Olde
Towne, but he had "decided not to embarrass them" by being turned
down. He had, however, formally applied for membership in the Twin
City Club because he believed a lot of lunchtime business transpired
there. He was rejected.

There is a similar absence of Jews in certain residential areas. Not
unexpectedly, these are the exclusive neighborhoods adjacent to the
country clubs. Except for these few areas, the Winston-Salem respondents indicated that there were neither "Jewish neighborhoods" nor
neighborhoods that excluded Jews. They were not sure that the lack of
Jews in the neighborhoods near the country clubs was completely a result
of exclusionary practices. One Jewish respondent told us that she had
almost bought a house near the entrance of one of the clubs, but decided

it would be "awkward" and "embarrassing" to live so close to the entrance of a club that would not accept her, surrounded by neighbors who were members of that club. In contrast, all the exclusive neighborhoods in Greensboro include Jewish residents.

Some of the Jewish residents of Winston-Salem are convinced that the failure of the broader community to accept Jews not only limits their activities, but also affects their children and the reactions of newcomers to the city. As one woman put it:

> In Winston-Salem if someone steps out of the Jewish community to take part in traditionally non-Jewish activities, they react as if you'd lost your mind. I think this kind of anti-Semitism is the reason so many of our children move out of town or marry non-Jews, and a lot of the younger Jewish couples who come to town don't stay very long.

Those who grew up in Winston-Salem were aware that things were different 20 miles east in Greensboro. It was considered "easier" there and, because the Jewish community was larger, "You had much more choice there—lots of nice eligible young Jewish boys." Similarly, the gentiles are aware of the reputation of their town on this score. As one put it: "I've discovered that Winston-Salem doesn't have a very good reputation for absorbing Jewish residents."

The extent to which Jews are excluded from Winston-Salem's social elite was indicated by numerous anecdotes in the interviews. One particularly telling story concerned a prominent gentile woman whose family was a member of the Forsyth Country Club. When she was engaged to marry a non-Jewish member of the wealthy Greensboro Cone family (a man who had been raised as an Episcopalian), her family attempted to arrange the reception at the country club. They were told they could not have it there "because he was Jewish." Though his mother was Episcopalian, and he had been raised as an Episcopalian, his father was Jewish and his name was Cone.

There is an interesting corporate footnote to the Winston-Salem story. In 1978, Hanes Underwear—corporate bastion of the Winston-Salem Protestant Establishment, controlled by a third generation of Hanes who had been educated at elite prep schools such as Woodberry Forest and Phillips Andover—was purchased against the will of the Hanes Family. Consolidated Food Corporation used $250 million to buy enough Hanes stock in a ten-day period to leave the Hanes management with no option but to be bought out. So Hanes, the developer of L'eggs Pantyhose, became part of the Chicago-based corporate giant. The founder of Consolidated Foods and the man who masterminded this and numerous other corporate purchases, was 82-year-old Nathan

Cummings, an Eastern European Jew who ca[...] Canada in 1939, did not graduate from colleg[...] Consolidated Foods until 1947.

CONCLUSIONS

It is our belief that the striking differences we [...] Greensboro and Winston-Salem may be to a larg[...] differing economic histories of the two towns [...] influential presence in Greensboro of one fami[...] have played a crucial role in the apparent acce[...] higher social circles of that community. Becaus[...] ficance to the city of Cone Mills when the var[...] clubs began, prominent Jews, among them mem[...] were among the charter members. With such e[...] vided by the Cones, and by other wealthy Jewi[...] have been "absorbed" quite well into most seg[...] of Greensboro.

The situation was and is different in Wir[...] Jews who "did well" in Winston-Salem early in t[...] approached the economic clout of the Greensb[...] class non-Jewish woman who has lived in bot[...] mented: "The difference between the two citie[...] to the Cones, the Sternbergers and others wh[...] Winston-Salem it was a Protestant gang in co[...]

There are, however, other differences be[...] might have contributed to the differential tre[...] long-time presence in Greensboro of several [...] universities that have provided a more li[...] atmosphere than in Winston-Salem. In contra[...] university in Winston-Salem, was moved [...] Durham by the Reynolds Foundation, and is p[...] conservative southern Baptists. Another f[...] fluenced Greensboro's openness to Jews is t[...] Quakers in Greensboro. In their historic com[...] they too have contributed to the more lib[...] Guilford College in 1837, and actively partici[...] Railroad that helped slaves escape to the No[...]

Putting aside the question of differences[...] to city and region to region, the Jews of Gre[...] Cone family, have provided us with anot[...] assimilation of Jews into the Protestant Esta[...]

few [...]
hav[...]
late [...]
in G[...]
Jews[...]
less [...]

the [...]
succ[...]
pora[...]
not [...]

Chapter 5

Identity and Class
in
the Corporate Elite

In this final chapter, it will be our purpose to assess the relative importance of Jewish identity and class identity in those Jews who have become members of the corporate and social elites. As Jews have moved into these elites, has the nature of their Jewish identity changed? How have their experiences in elite institutions affected the way they present themselves and think of themselves? More specifically, have they become identified with the Protestant Establishment to such an extent that their assimilation contradicts Baltzell's fear that discrimination has led to a decline in the establishment's power and authority?

Identity is most simply defined as the answer to the question, Who Are You? (Vander Zanden, 1977: 75; Bugental and Zelen, 1950; Kuhn and McPartland, 1954). When the question is asked of Americans, several answers are likely to be forthcoming, for people's identities are complex mosaics that include several different and often conflicting components. Psychologists and psychoanalysts emphasize the personal sense of identity, especially the feeling that one is a unique human being possessing his or her own inherent characteristics, strengths and preferences; they put particular stress on the development of identity during childhood and adolescence (e.g., Erickson, 1950, 1958, 1968). Social psychologists and sociologists, on the other hand, tend to emphasize social identity, the ways in which people define themselves in terms of groups. A classic work of this genre (Hyman, 1942) suggested the term "reference group" to include those groups to which people may or may not belong, but, in either case, use as a means of self-appraisal and self-definition in developing their social identity.

When Americans are asked "Who Are You?" answers are likely to come in the following order: I am Joe Smith or Rachel Goldsmith; I am a man or woman; I am an American (perhaps adding, and proud of it); I am a lawyer; and I am a Protestant or Catholic or Jew. Depending on how many generations their families have lived in this country, they may or may not say that they are Irish, or Scottish, or a Russian Jew. If pushed, they may add that they are Southerners or Californians or New Yorkers. Whatever the exact order of these usual answers, the typical person is unlikely to say that "I am a member of the upper class" or "I am a member of the working class" (Kahl, 1959: 157). In that sense, Americans do not use class as a reference group.

Although there were clear class distinctions among people in terms of wealth, income, occupation, and life style at the time America won its independence, the evidence from newspapers, diaries, and letters of that period suggests that most Americans did not think in terms of class even then because they believed classes to be much less important in the New World than in the more rigid class system that existed in Europe (Main, 1965). More salient to the citizens of the 1770s was the idea that America was "the land of opportunity," at least for those not part of the slave caste, whose existence was ignored in making these general claims. Two hundred years later, a representative sample of Americans from all levels of the income ladder in Boston and Kansas City were saying the same thing to sociologists in survey interviews. People believe that class is of little—and declining—importance in the United States because, in the summary words of social science, there is social mobility and a formal system of equality (Coleman and Rainwater, 1978).

The reluctance of Americans to use class as a reference group has led survey researchers to rely on a forced-choice format when asking questions about class. As Mayer and Buckley (1969: 131–32) write in their overview of research on social class, "The widespread reluctance to recognize or admit the existence of classes and the persistence of the American dream of equality of opportunity require a forced-choice question to induce many, perhaps most, Americans to identify themselves with their objective class position." Thus, when sociologists at the University of Michigan's Institute for Social Research have asked their question about social class for the past 30 years, they have asked it in two stages. First, "Do you ever think of yourself as belonging in one of these classes?" If the respondent says either "No" or "I don't know," as about one-third do, the surveyor asks them what they would say if they had to make a choice (Hamilton, 1972: 100–101; Converse, Dotson, Hoag, and McGee, 1980: 22).

Even those in the social upper class, the group most likely to admit to class membership according to several studies (Lipset and Bendix, 1951: 249), do not like to speak about the class structure. "One does not speak of classes; they are felt," was the acid comment of an upper-class "matron" in a study of class identification in New Haven, Connecticut (Hollingshead and Redlich, 1958: 69). More recently, when sociologist Susan A. Ostrander (1980: 79) asked 38 upper-class women at the end of a long interview whether or not they would consider themselves members of the upper class, most of them rejected the idea with comments such as the following:

> I hate [the term] "upper class." It's so non-upper class to use it. I just call it "all of us," those of us who are wellborn.

> I wouldn't classify anyone as upper class, just as productive, worthwhile people.

> I'd prefer to think of it as established, of a certain economic group of social status.

> I hate to use the word "class." We're responsible, fortunate people, old families, the people who have something.

An anecdote told by Marietta Peabody Tree, an upper-class woman from Boston "brahmins" who married into the British aristocracy, makes the same point in a more dramatic fashion. She recalls that her "first and only" slap from her grandmother came when as a child she referred to an acquaintance as "very middle class." "After the slap came these stern, grandmotherly words: there are no classes in America—upper, middle, or lower. You are never to use that term again" (Birmingham, 1958: 340).

Nonetheless, when it comes to categories such as "big businessman" or "upper class," most people know there is a "they" that does not include them. In one of the classic questionnaire studies on class identification (Centers, 1949:80–3, 94–5), 82 percent of the respondents said that big businessmen were part of an upper class, and only 3 percent of those who called themselves middle class and 0.2 percent of those who called themselves working class claimed that big businessmen were part of their class. Similarly, a study of Kansas City residents in the early 1950s found that people "at all levels of Kansas City life" volunteered the belief that there was an upper class in Kansas City even though they didn't use that term: "Each person had his own favorite phrase for people at the top, but the most common were 'the big rich,' 'the bluebloods,' 'the bankers and lawyers,' 'people who live in the mansions out Southwest,' and 'those people in the elite country clubs'" (Coleman and Neugarten, 1971: 16). Another sociologist, Paul Blumberg (1980: 54), puts it this way: "Although explicit class terms are generally avoided on the level of everyday discourse, American thought and language is suffused with thinly masked but universally understood euphemisms that carry concrete expressions of social class, social distance, and social mobility: high society; upper crust; higher ups; the other side of the tracks; making good; rags to riches; social climber; moving up in the world; keeping up with the Joneses; poor but honest; white trash; ne'er-do-well; and dozens more. In fact, social class is the essence of what most Americans mean when they speak of personal success or failure." When pressed a little bit, some members of the upper class will agree that they are part of such a class. One woman told Ostrander (1980: 78) at the end of an interview: "We're not supposed to have layers. I'm embarrassed to admit to you that we do, and that I feel superior at my social level. I like being part of the upper crust."

However, as Ostrander (1980: 87–88) emphasizes, the class identity of her upper-class respondents was most likely to reveal itself "in terms of class-related behaviors and values," in a feeling, for example, that volunteer work in the community "ought" to be done; or that a debut was necessary for the sake of the family and tradition; or that private schools should be attended so that children would learn the "proper" ways to behave and make the right kinds of contacts. Discussion of social club membership was especially informative on this issue. It was necessary that they be by-invitation-only so that not "just anybody" could be around when you want to relax with people who are like you—people who are "congenial" and "compatible." Most of her subjects went on to suggest that it is a good idea for potential club members to be "sponsored" by people who are well known and trusted by everyone, which is evidence, Ostrander argues, that the people she interviewed were very class conscious in the sense that they all knew "what upper-class persons are expected to *do* to maintain the boundaries of class association."

Upper-class identity, then, usually will not be found in the spontaneous assertion that "I am a member of the upper crust," but in statements about values and behavior in relation to specific institutions of the class, such as schools and clubs. It is on this level that class as a reference group is revealed by euphemisms such as the "best" neighborhoods, the "proper" schools, the "compatible" clubs, and the "right" families.

JEWISH IDENTITY

Just as class identity is best understood in relation to specific social institutions, so, too, is Jewish identity best understood through such reference groups as religious institutions, clubs, and other social organizations that are Jewish. Some scholars have argued that there is an important difference between "Jewish identity" and "Jewish identification." "Identity" refers to what being Jewish means to people in terms of their self-definition. "Identification" refers to forms of involvement (such as memberships in Jewish organizations, or participation in certain ritual behaviors) and the extent to which people adopt these various forms. Whereas Herman (1977: 28) is critical of the extensiveness of the research on Jewish identification and the lack of it on Jewish identity, Harold Himmelfarb (1980: 50) takes the opposite position. It is his view that "Scholars have been concentrating on the more significant phenomenon. Studies of identification, rather than identity, are those most likely to yield information about Jewish life." In our view, Himmelfarb is correct. Jewish identification is not only easier to assess, but it allows for an objective evaluation of a person's reference groups which, in turn, can be used to draw inferences about Jewish identity.

Though Jewish identification may be easier to assess than Jewish identity, there is no single way to assess it that has been accepted by all. Himmelfarb is but one of an increasing number of scholars who have developed measures of Jewish identification. He suggests that religious identification has four general orientations (the supernatural, the communal, the cultural, and the interpersonal), and proposes a model consisting of nine dimensions and three subdimensions designed to provide empirical data on each of the four general orientations. Using a factor analysis of data gathered on a sample of Jewish adults, he suggests that religious involvement for Jews is based on different dimensions than it is for Christians (Himmelfarb, 1975). Others have suggested other models, with other orientations or dimensions. Bock (1976) suggests ten dimensions of Jewish identification; Lazerwitz (1973) proposes eight; and Verbit (1970) presents six "components" of Jewish identification.

In his review article on the topic, Himmelfarb (1980: 51) points out that all four of these models tend to agree on the following seven dimensions (that is, each of the following appears in at least three of the models): (1) ritual behavior; (2) formal organizational participation; (3) informal social ties with other Jews (friends, neighbors, mates); (4) positive attitudes toward Israel; (5) doctrinal belief; (6) some intellectual dimension; and (7) some measure of charity-giving.

Himmelfarb (1980: 52) also mentions that "the simplest and most efficient indicator of overall Jewish identification might well be denominational self-identification." On every dimension of Jewish identification, there is a clear rank ordering pattern in which the Orthodox Jews score highest, the Conservative Jews score next highest, the Reform Jews score third highest, and the nondenominational Jews score lowest.

The multidimensional models are, we believe, useful for studies in which there is the opportunity for detailed analysis, including paper and pencil testing, of the religious views and experiences of large groups of subjects. However, they were inappropriate for our needs with a small interview sample. Similarly, the unidimensional measure of denominational affiliation is a useful indicator of Jewish identification for some samples, but since almost all of the Jews in this study are at least nominally members of Reform congregations, it was not sufficient for our purposes. We needed something less comprehensive than the multidimensional scales reviewed by Himmelfarb, and something more comprehensive than denominational affiliation. As Himmelfarb (1975: 614) himself said, "Religious involvement can be measured in many different ways but probably only some of the ways are relevant to each study."

The method we chose was stimulated by a study done in 1933 by C. Luther Fry on "The Religious Affiliations of American Leaders." Fry found, among other things, that only 218 of the 29,623 people in the 1930–31 edition of Who's Who in America claimed to be Jewish. This figure, a mere 0.74 percent of the total, was considerably smaller than the percentage of Jews in the population at large, and this underrepresentation contrasted strikingly with the frequency figures for various other denominational groups.

Fry then turned to two other sources: Who's Who in American Jewry and the American Jewish Yearbook. He looked up those people listed in the two sources who also were included in Who's Who in America. He found 650 such individuals, of whom only 218 identified themselves, in Who's Who in America, as being Jewish (432 people omitted the fact that they were Jewish). Fry concluded that "certain individuals may hesitate to classify themselves as Jews because such an admission would be considered a social liability" (Fry, 1933:246).

As Fry's study suggests, there is considerable latitude in the kinds of information people choose to include in their Who's Who in America biographies. Although the publishers provide a basic format with 18 categories, many people choose to include information on some but not all of the categories. For example, almost all of the people in Who's Who in America give their year of birth (under category #3, "vital statistics"), but some women and older people do not. Many people include their religion (category #14), but over the past forty years, more and more have chosen to omit this information. Some reveal that they are in certain clubs (category #5), but others (such as Ronald Reagan and George Bush in the case of San Francisco's Bohemian Club) do not. People can admit to their "Political Affiliations" (category #13), and they can inform the journalists, scholars, and corporate publicists who use the Who's Who in America for reference purposes that they won a particular tennis tournament or outstanding business leadership award (category #11, "Awards and Certifications").

For our purposes, the crucial point about the personal selectivity that goes into including or omitting certain information is that the biographical sketches can be seen as a reflection of how various people choose to present themselves to public view (Goffman, 1959). Thus, the biographical sketches not only provide useful information about a Jewish person's identification with the religion, and with particular reference groups, but they also allow inferences to be made about that person's Jewish identity. It is in this context that we followed Fry's lead and used *Who's Who in America* as an unobtrusive source for the measurement of Jewish identification.

Our interest was primarily in whether or not Jews revealed themselves as being Jewish in their biographical sketches, and the manner in which they did so. The most direct way they could indicate that they were Jewish was to include "Jewish" or "Jewish religion" at category #14 (as one-third of Frey's sample did). We therefore assigned this as the strongest indication of Jewish identification. If people did not state directly that they were Jewish, but did include affiliations with one or more clearly Jewish organization (such as B'nai B'rith, the American Jewish Committee, or the United Jewish Appeal), we assigned them to our second category of Jewish identification. If people did not qualify for either of the first two categories, but did include membership in one or more clubs known by us to be primarily Jewish in their membership (such as New York's Harmonie Club or Los Angeles' Hillcrest Country Club), we assigned them to the third category. Finally, if they did not list that they were Jewish and gave no indication of Jewish affiliations, they were placed in the fourth category. The scale, then, included the following four categories:

1. "Jewish religion"
2. Jewish organization(s)
3. Jewish club(s)
4. None

We looked up the more than 3,000 members of the Harmonie Club (1977-78), the Standard Club (1977-78), and the Hillcrest Country Club (1974-75) and found 351 who also appeared in the corresponding editions of *Who's Who in America*. We rated these 351 individuals on our four-point scale of Jewish identification. In addition, we recorded each person's corporate directorships and, having confirmed these in *Moody's* or *Standard and Poor's*, we were able to compare the *Fortune*-level directors with the nondirectors. Our findings, which can be seen in Table 5.1, show that slightly more than half (49 of 90, or 54 percent) of the corporate directors who were members of one or more of these three clubs were in

TABLE 5.1.
Jewish Identification of Members of the Harmonie, Hillcrest, and
Standard Clubs Whose Names Appeared in *Who's Who in America*

	Directors			*Nondirectors*		
	All	*Born before 1910*	*Born 1910 or later*	*All*	*Born before 1910*	*Born 1910 or later*
Category 1	13	5	8	53	17	36
Category 2	28	11	17	87	35	52
Category 3	25	3	22	70	27	43
Category 4	24	3	21	51	24	27
Total	90	22	68	261	103	158

one of the two categories indicating the lowest levels of Jewish identification ("Jewish club" or "none"). In contrast, slightly less than half (121 of 261, or 46 percent) of the club members who were not *Fortune*-level directors fell in one of these two categories. These data suggested that the directors were less likely than the nondirectors to present themselves as Jewish, but the differences were slight (and not statistically significant).

However, a significant pattern emerged when the age of the various club members was taken into account. There was a clear tendency for the younger club members who are corporate directors to reveal their Jewishness in *Who's Who in America* only through their club memberships or not at all. Whereas only 27 percent of the corporate directors in these three clubs who were born before 1910 fell into categories 3 and 4, the corresponding figure for those born in 1910 or later was 63 percent. This was not the pattern for the nondirectors: they were no more likely to fall in categories 3 and 4 (in fact 88 of the 158, or 56 percent, fell in categories 1 or 2).*

These data were corroborated by a study we did of the 1978 Board of Governors of the American Jewish Committee in which we looked to see if the 49 members who appeared in *Who's Who in America* had included their AJC affiliation in their biographical sketches. We found that 76 percent of those who were not corporate directors included their AJC affiliation, but only 45 percent of those who were corporate directors included it.*

---

*See Appendix 2 for a version of this paragraph that includes tests of statistical significance.

The analyses we just have described indicate that members of three prominent Jewish clubs, and the board members of a prestigious Jewish civic organization, are less likely to reveal their Jewish identity in *Who's Who in America* if they are corporate directors as well. This is especially true for younger directors. But the large number of Jewish organizations listed by directors and nondirectors that fell into the second category of our scale, "Jewish organizations," suggested the need to perform an additional analysis of the kinds of Jewish organizations that Jewish directors do include in their biographical sketches. Are certain kinds of Jewish organizations more likely than others to serve as reference groups for Jewish directors in the corporate elite?

THE JEWISH AFFILIATIONS OF JEWISH CORPORATE DIRECTORS

To answer this question, we turned to our sample of 219 Jews drawn from the *Trustees of Wealth*, the "who's who" of American philanthropy. As we said in the second chapter, we selected these Jewish trustees on the basis of their having indicated affiliations with Jewish organizations or clubs in their biographical sketches. We can now consider what those particular affiliations were, and see whether or not those Jewish trustees who also were corporate directors were more likely to belong to some organizations than others.

Table 5.2 includes those Jewish organizations in which at least five Jewish foundation trustees had listed membership. These organizations are listed with those that had the highest percentage of corporate directors (among the Jewish trustees who indicated membership) at the top, and those that had the lowest percentage at the bottom. As can be seen, three of the top six are primarily academic in nature (the American Friends of Hebrew University, Albert Einstein Medical College, and Brandeis University) and two are primarily fund raising organizations (Council of Jewish Federations and Welfare Boards, and the United Jewish Appeal). This suggests that Jews involved in the highest levels of corporate power, if they are in Jewish organizations at all, are more likely to report being involved in those which focus on the philanthropic and the "cultural" rather than the religious aspects of Judaism.

In order to understand the role these organizations play in the lives of Jewish corporate directors, and more broadly, to understand the nature of their Jewish identity, let us now turn to our interview data. What did the corporate directors we spoke with say about being Jewish?

TABLE 5.2.
**Fortune Board Representation of Jewish Trustees of Wealth
Who List Memberships in Jewish Organizations**

Associations	N	One or More Fortune Boards	Percentage
Council of Jewish Federations and Welfare Board	6	4	66.7
American Friends of Hebrew Univ.	5	3	60.0
Albert Einstein Medical College	11	5	45.4
United Jewish Appeal	13	4	30.8
Jewish Community Centers	7	2	28.6
Brandeis Univ.	15	4	26.7
Anti-Defamation League	6	1	16.7
Federation of Jewish Philanths.	22	2	9.1
National Jewish Welfare Board	13	1	7.7
American Jewish Committee	13	0	0
Hebrew Union College	9	0	0
National Conf. Christians and Jews	6	0	0
American Jewish Congress	5	0	0
Jewish Federation	5	0	0
	135	26	19.2

"JEWISH BUT NOT RELIGIOUS"

Many of the corporate directors whom we interviewed identified themselves very strongly as Jewish, but few viewed themselves as religious. Very few indicated that they go to a synagogue or temple other than during the High Holidays, and many indicated that they don't attend at all. The response of Witco Chemical's William Wishnick to our question about what being Jewish meant to him was informative: "I can tell you what it doesn't mean: It doesn't mean going to temple twice a year. I don't think it's important to go twice a year, on Rosh Hashonah and Yom Kippur, to show you're a good Jew." Others who do attend services twice a year were likely to say, in one way or another, that their sense of being Jewish was not manifested through involvement with the synagogue or temple. Even Laurence Tisch (referred to by many we spoke

with as one of the Jewish corporate leaders most active in Jewish community affairs, and a person adamant in his belief that "Jews be identified
as Jews and be strong in their convictions as Jews") was quick to dis-
tinguish between being Jewish and being religious: "I'm not really involved in synagogue affairs. I'm on the board of the Jewish Theological
Seminary, but I'm not a religious person as such."

Our interviews underscored our finding that for Jews in the corporate elite, philanthropy, and fundraising represented the primary
means of demonstrating commitment to being Jewish. All of those we
spoke with, even those who have not been inside a synagogue or temple
in years, contribute to Jewish causes. Some went so far as to indicate
that they had returned to involvement in the Jewish community through
the avenue of fundraising. Until they started raising money, they had
avoided coming to terms with their Jewishness. As one such person
said, "In college the last thing I did was to be involved with Jews or Jewish
things." Another referred to his earlier avoidance of contact with Jewish
activities, and with the entire issue of Jewish identity, by saying, "I
ducked it." But for a variety of reasons—including anti-Semitic incidents,
events in Israel, and a feeling of obligation to provide leadership in the
community—they became more involved in Jewish affairs. Invariably,
this took the form of fundraising and philanthropy. In no case did it entail
regular attendance at religious services or frequent participation in
religious rituals.

Fundraising and philanthropy are not only important activities in
the Jewish community, they are highly regarded activities in corporate
circles as well, and are even thought by some observers to be required for
corporate advancement and acceptance into the social elite. Furthermore,
raising money for Jewish causes sometimes leads to fundraising for the
broader community. More than one director mentioned to us that after
years of fundraising for UJA, or the local Federation, they had become
actively involved in raising money for the United Fund. When this
occurred, as one put it, "I had to ease off on the Federation for a while."
Raising money for the United Fund not only benefits local community
services such as YMCAs, community hotlines, and centers for retarded
children, but it also may benefit the corporate leaders raising the money.
As Peter Haas of Levi Strauss candidly said of his work with the United
Fund: "That's the springboard for meeting an awful lot of people around
town. That opened up a lot of contacts." Joseph N. Mitchell of Los
Angeles, the head of a family insurance company not quite large enough
to be in the Fortune top 50, told us that his fundraising work in the Jewish
community in the 1960s led to his heading up the United Way campaign
in 1972. This, in turn, led to a "personal friendship" with the chairman of
Pacific Lighting, the 48th largest utility in 1981, and Mitchell's subsequent appointment to the board.

Thus, involvement in Jewish fundraising allows Jews in the corporate elite to identify with their Jewishness in a way that often leads to increased contact with their gentile counterparts. And, as Charles Liebman points out in his *The Ambivalent American Jew* (1973: 103), such fundraising allows for "an outlet and expression of Jewish activity which is religiously legitimate, but which is entirely secular in content," and it allows the person "to do what he excels at—fund raising and organization."

Fundraising and Jewishness interact in another secular arena, politics, where many Jews are major fundraisers for both political parties. Although they have been most prominent within the Democratic Party over the past fifty years—perhaps beginning with Sidney Weinberg's role as an assistant treasurer for the party in 1932 and continuing through 1968 when Jews provided half or more of the large gifts that went to Hubert Humphrey's presidential bid—they have become increasingly identified with the Republicans as well. The Republican identification, already present in about half of all large Jewish donors in the 1960s but not highly visible because of the overwhelming gentile presence in that party, was increased in the 1970s because of the Jewish fundraisers' dislike for George McGovern's extreme liberalism and his ambiguity concerning Israel.

Stephen D. Isaacs, a journalist for *The Washington Post*, opens his book on *Jews and American Politics* (1974: 1-2) by describing a dramatic scene early in 1970 in which McGovern met with 39 Jewish "financial giants" at a luncheon arranged by Laurence Tisch as a favor to his friend Henry Kimmelman, McGovern's "financial chief and principal angel." McGovern gave an unsatisfactory answer to the first question ("Senator, just what is your position on Israel?"), by stressing the role of the United Nations. According to Isaacs: "With that answer, McGovern blew most of the traditional big money from Jews in 1972, money that was to go first to Hubert Humphrey, then later into the Republican campaign in unprecedented amounts." According to one man present, McGovern's mention of the United Nations "was like waving a red flag in front of a bull."

One of the directors we talked to acknowledged this shift toward the Republicans, and defended it by saying, "Republicans have been good to Israel. The best friend Israel ever had was Nixon."

But Israel is not the only issue of interest to Jews when judging politicians. After conducting hundreds of interviews, Isaacs concluded that the most important reason for the involvement of Jews in politics is the fear that "it"—with "it" never having to be defined—could happen here: "Fear undoubtedly is the greatest single factor accounting for Jews' high level of political activity" (Isaacs, 1974: 15). They work to keep the system as open and unprejudiced as possible so it will remain "free from the terrors that almost all other systems before have meant for the Jews" (1974: 25).

The high level of concern with anti-Semitism in American politics is revealed in an unusual ad purchased during the 1980 presidential campaign by Arnold M. Picker. Picker, a former top executive with United Artists, was one of the major fundraisers and contributors for Democrats in the 1960s and early 1970s, lending Humphrey $100,000 in 1968 and contributing about $260,000 to the primary campaign of Edmund Muskie in 1972 (Isaacs, 1974: 121; Alexander, 1976: 136). In 1976, Picker raised money for Jimmy Carter, but in 1980 he spent money to defeat him, and the switchover was in good part due to the issue of anti-Semitism.

The money to defeat Carter was spent on a full-page ad he took out in the *Miami Herald*, (1980: 2-D). It reprinted an open letter to Jimmy Carter from Morris B. Abram, one of the most respected members of the Jewish community in America. A former president of Brandeis University, and now a partner in the Wall Street law firm of Paul, Weiss, Rifkind, Wharton and Garrison, the Atlanta-born Abram was an enthusiastic supporter of Carter in 1976, but came to be increasingly dismayed by Carter's performance in office on the question of anti-Semitism. The fact that Carter did not publicly rebuke his brother Billy for his repeated anti-Semitic remarks finally led Abram to open opposition. He wrote a scathing letter to Carter which *The New York Times* refused to print. The letter then appeared in *The New York Post* (October 31, 1980), and it gained further public attention when Picker bought the ad that publicized Abram's views. It was titled "The President's Flabby Stand on Anti-Semitism," and it read in part:

> It is widely recognized that the President's failure as a moral leader is reflected in his steady retreat from a campaign pledge of absolute truthfulness. I am even more disappointed, however, by Mr. Carter's inadequate response to the overt anti-Semitism of certain of his closest relatives and friends. ...
>
> On February 15, 1979, at a dinner at Atlanta, I stated that the social taboo that once restrained most people against public expressions of anti-Semitism appeared to be weakening.
>
> Even the brother of the President has given public aid and comfort to the envoys of Libya while himself uttering the remarks that are not laughable or clownish—or just merely vulgar—but dangerous anti-Semitic canards.
>
> That very night, in New York, the President's brother confirmed my worst suspicions by announcing that the Jewish community "can kiss my ass."
>
> Mr. Carter has encouraged his brother's mercenary dealings with

Libya, and employed him as a contact with this most viciously anti-Semitic and terrorist of regimes.

Less blatant, but perhaps of more lasting significance, was Mr. Carter's failure for over a month to set the record straight on the reasons for the resignation of Ambassador Young.

By refusing to admit that Young had been dismissed for cause—for insubordination and submission of disingenuous reports to the State Department—Mr. Carter encouraged suspicions that the Jewish community and Israel were somehow to blame.

One can sense the depth of Abram's feelings in this break from his fellow Georgian and Democrat. Abram took this strong stand against Carter, and by implication, for Ronald Reagan, for the same reason that led Communist Party member Peggy Dennis to proclaim, "While anti-Semitism and ethnic discrimination exist anywhere, I am a Jew" (Dennis, 1980: 48).

The persistence of anti-Semitism is, of course, the reason many Jews think full assimilation is an unreachable dream. "Who knows how many hundreds and maybe even thousands of years it's going to take, if ever it does disappear?" asked Joseph Cullman. "When Hitler came around he didn't ask questions whether you were or you weren't—it wasn't what you said, it was what he said," said Laurence Tisch. Both Cullman and Tisch's comments, as was also true in the statements just cited by Morris Abram and Peggy Dennis, acknowledge that as long as the possibility of anti-Semitism persists, being Jewish must be a part of their self-identity.

And, just as the issue of anti-Semitism is at the core of Jewish identity, so too is the issue of Israel. Israel is more than just the primary location of a religious and cultural heritage. It speaks to a collective past as a once-united people within a nation-state, one that was defeated and dispersed, but one that has lived on in cultural tradition. The depth of Jewish ties to Israel can be seen in the 2000-year quest that kept alive the hope of returning to the homeland (the traditional seder ends with the wish, "Next year in Jerusalem"); these deep feelings only were reinforced by centuries of anti-Semitic pogroms and the still vivid Nazi holocaust that killed 6 million Jews, while the United States and other nations kept their borders closed to large numbers of possible Jewish immigrants and tried not to face "the terrible secret" (Lacqueur, 1980).

As powerful as the Israel issue is, however, it has not reached so deeply that very many American Jews have wanted to go to this homeland. Between 1948 and 1968, a mere 20,000 American Jews left to settle there, and for every ten that went, nine returned to the United States. In 1973, only 4,176 Jews from North America (including Canada) moved to Israel (Isaacs, 1974: 253). As sociologist Chaim Waxman has stressed, American Jews are "overwhelmingly pro-Israel" but very few are Zionists (1976: 177).

The survival of Israel, then, has been an extremely powerful element in the identity of American Jews. In fact, Nathan Glazer (1979: 233) goes so far as to claim that "Israel has become *the* Jewish religion for American Jews." But American Jews have remained, first and foremost, Americans. And, as Israel becomes more independent and distinctive in her style and policies, American Jews view themselves as more and more different from Israeli Jews even while their emotional involvement in providing support for Israel remains a central factor in their identity as Jews.

Most fundraising in the Jewish community, then, is not primarily for local charities, or for the Democrats, or even to defend against anti-Semitism in America: it is for Israel. The United Jewish Appeal, the Federations, and other fundraising groups provide a tremendous amount of money for the support of Israel. Waxman (1976: 175) points out that "thirty-five of the largest and most active of the national organizations are affiliated with the Conference of Presidents of Major American Jewish Organizations, for which Zionist and pro-Israel activity is the major emphasis."

Although all the corporate directors we spoke with indicated that they give regularly to Jewish charities, their involvement with Israel varied tremendously. For the most part, they fell into one of two groups. The first consists of those who not only give money, but who are also deeply involved in fundraising and in Israel as a personal, emotional issue. As one director who is extremely active in fundraising frankly stated, "To me Israel is an emotional thing, not a political thing." Without exception, the directors who fell into this first group were born in Eastern Europe, or their parents were born in Eastern Europe. The second group consisted of those who give money but are not active in fundraising and are not particularly emotionally involved with Israel. This group, without exception, consisted of the descendants of German Jews who had come to America in the middle of the nineteenth century and a few third-generation Eastern European Jews whose grandparents arrived before the turn of the century. As one of these third-generation Eastern European Jews said when asked about his feelings toward Israel, "I'm a supporter, but not an ardent supporter. I give my money but I don't give myself." Or, as one of the German Jews put it, "You know, you sort of root for them," but, "I don't feel that Israel is my country right or wrong."

These two groups—the more recently successful first and second generation Eastern European Jews and the older-monied German Jews, along with a few third-generation, older-monied Eastern European Jews —differed on a number of issues related to Israel. The fact that the older-monied, third-generation Eastern European Jews responded more like the German Jews than like the first or second-generation Eastern European Jews on these various issues reinforces our belief that as far as Jewish identity goes, the key variable is how long one's family has been in the corporate elite, not whether one is an Eastern European or German Jew. Accordingly, we will discuss the differences between these two groups as between more recent arrivals to the corporate elite (all of whom are of Eastern European descent) and longer-term members of the corporate elite (most of whom are of German descent, but some of whom are Eastern European).

Indeed, we think the traditional distinction between German and Eastern European Jews is now irrelevant and misleading, and it may always have been in terms of acceptance into the very highest levels of society and business. The more important distinction depends upon the generation in which the family gained its wealth, just as it does with members of other ethnic and religious groups. In this regard, it is noteworthy that almost half of the successful Jewish business people we interviewed turned out to be Eastern European Jews. We do not know if these figures reflect broader patterns in clubs and on boards of directors, for we were only able to determine these details of family background for those we interviewed. It was clear, however, that on several issues those Eastern-European Jews whose grandparents had arrived early in the wave of Eastern European immigration—the 1880s—responded more like German Jews than like the Eastern European Jews whose families came to America closer to or after the turn of the century.

First of all, the more recent arrivals to the corporate elite were much more likely than the longer-term members to have visited Israel. Most of them, like Sam Stroum of Seattle, indicated they had been to Israel "many times," and a few specified exactly how many times ("twenty-six times" said one) or how recently they had been there ("Just returned a few weeks ago," said another). In striking contrast, many of the longer-term members of the corporate elite had never been to Israel, and those who had been there had visited once or twice. Joseph F. Cullman 3rd, whose German-Jewish grandfather had started a tobacco company in the 1870s that was later to buy out Benson and Hedges, told us that although he had traveled all over the world, and has supported Israel "financially and emotionally, it just happens that I haven't been there." John Weinberg, who attended Deerfield, Princeton, and Harvard, told us: I've not been there. I've given money to some of the Jewish causes, and I've supported them. And I respect the people who do, but I feel more myself as an American." And Jay Pritzker told us that when he was 11 years old, his wealthy Eastern European grandfather (who had a major influence on him) took him out of the private school he was attending so that he could accompany him on a six-month trip around the world. On that trip they visited Israel—at the time it was still Palestine—and he has been back twice, both brief visits on his way to other places (as he put it, "I've been there but not really").

At the time of our New York and Boston interviews, conducted in the summer of 1980, a full-page ad had appeared in *The New York Times* that criticized Israeli Prime Minister Menachem Begin's policies of continued settlements on the West Bank. The ad had been signed by 90 sponsors, including association executives, authors, playwrights, lawyers, and Nobel laureates. We asked each of the New York and Boston directors if they had been approached to sign the ad, and if they thought it was appropriate for American Jews to criticize Israeli policies in such a public manner. Invariably, the longer-term members of the corporate elite had not been approached, but saw nothing wrong with American Jews making their views known in such a way. As one of them responded when asked if he had any qualms about American Jews making such a public critique, "Hell, no. I'm an American citizen, first and foremost, Jewish by ethnic background or whatever you want to call it, but I'm supporting, I feel for, the United States of America."

In contrast, the more recent arrivals to the corporate elite stressed they did not agree with Begin on everything (indeed, some disagreed vehemently with him on many things), but they would not participate in that kind of public break with Israeli policy. The response of Simon Rifkind was not atypical: "I thought it was an imprudent thing. They're entitled to do it if they want to do it but I would not join it, let's put it just that way. If Mr. Begin sent for me and asked me to give him my reactions to what he was doing, I would give him my honest opinion. I did the same with David Ben-Gurion, but he did ask me, Begin hasn't asked me."

Laurence Tisch had this to say:

> That's such a tough issue. I'm openly critical in Jewish circles. I'm openly critical to Israelis. But I won't sign these public documents because I think that the average non-Jew doesn't understand—they take it as a renunciation of Israel more than a desire to see a change in the government. I don't think that the American Jewish community can afford to have the American government think that the Jews are not behind Israel. So though I'm very critical of Mr. Begin, I don't think it's my place to do it publicly.

Rifkind was not the only recent arrival to the corporate elite who mentioned that he had had direct contact with leading Israeli politicians. Just as he had been asked for his reactions by Ben-Gurion, others had been asked (or had decided to speak up even if not asked) about their reactions to other Israeli leaders. "I've spoken to Begin," said Laurence Tisch. "I've spoken to Dayan. I speak with the people involved." Preston Robert Tisch, the president of Loews, reiterated his brother Laurence's belief that American Jews have the right to criticize Israel, though they should use appropriate channels. "If we think they're doing something wrong," he told us, "we have the right to criticize. If we don't have the right to criticize, then we shouldn't have the right to support them."

The more recent arrivals to the corporate elite also mentioned working through particular channels to make their unhappiness known to Israeli leaders. One such channel is the American Jewish Committee, but its directors have been very reluctant to criticize Israeli policy. One recent arrival to the American corporate elite, who is active in the AJC, told us that at its last annual meeting, the AJC had adopted a statement "by a split vote in which there is a very mild, I wouldn't even call it a condemnatory, questioning of Israeli policy, along with an attack on Western Europe, and the Arabs, and everybody else. And even that took a big fight."

Writing on the question of Jewish identity and Israel, Liebman (1973: 90–92) suggests that every group or community has ways by which it distinguishes itself from the rest of society, and that there are certain positions on issues or behaviors that one must adhere to in order to continue to be accepted as part of the group. Such crucial issues, which determine the difference between acceptance and unacceptable deviance, he refers to as "boundary defining positions," and he asserts that "support for Israel . . . represents the crucial boundary today in the American Jewish community." As we have indicated, all of those we spoke with stayed on the acceptable side of this boundary by supporting Israel financially.

However, this "boundary defining position" of support for Israel was central to the identity of the more recent arrivals to the corporate elite, but relatively marginal to the identities of the longer-term members of the corporate elite. One longer-term member of the corporate elite went so far as to say that he only gave money to Israel and maintained a membership in a reform congregation because he was a "coward" and didn't want to deal with the scorn from the Jewish community were he to refuse to do so. Irving Rabb of Boston, an Eastern European Jew and a relative newcomer to the corporate elite as an owner and director of Stop and Shop (the 30th largest retail company in 1981), may have been correct when he said, bemoaning the loss of the feeling of "yiddishkeit" in America: "If it weren't for Israel, I think we'd be in trouble."

CLASS IDENTITY AT THE TOP?

Aside from the profoundly important issues of anti-Semitism and the defense of Israel, we believe that the primary identifications of successful

Jewish businessmen and their families are with the corporate and social elites, not with their Jewishness. Although Jewishness remains a meaningful part of their identity, even more important are their involvements with top-level social and corporate institutions. This shift from ethnic identity to a predominantly class identity is best captured in the phrase of sociologist Peter I. Rose (1981: 16), an expert on race and ethnicity in America. Rose calls such people JASPS, Jewish Anglo-Saxon Protestants; they are Jewish in the same way in which multimillionaire scion John F. Kennedy, a graduate of Choate and Harvard, was Irish:

> In most respects Kennedy departed considerably from the Irish American stereotype. He was reticent, patrician, bookish, urbane—much closer, indeed, to a young Lord Salisbury than to a young Al Smith or, for that matter, to a young John F. Fitzgerald [his maternal grandfather]. Yet the Irishness remained a vital element in his constitution (Schlesinger, 1965: 78).

Our argument on the importance of class identity to Jews in the Protestant Establishment starts with a definition of social class that puts its emphasis on social interactions as distinguishing criteria: "A social class," wrote sociologists A. Davis, B. B. Gardner, and M. R. Gardner (1941: 59) in their classic study of caste and class in the Deep South, "is the largest group of people whose members have intimate access to one another. A class is composed of families and social cliques. The interrelationships between these families and cliques, in such informal activities as dancing, visiting, receptions, teas, and larger informal affairs, constitute the structure of the social class."

The Jewish businessmen we have studied are part of the upper-class social elite with regard to all interactive criteria except membership in certain social clubs. We have seen that many attended the exclusive private preparatory schools of the upper class, which C. Wright Mills (1956: 64) goes so far as to say are the best "clue" to the "national unity of the upper social classes in America today." There is even more of a tendency for their children to attend these schools; this is true for both newer and older members of the corporate elite. The same findings hold for the college level, where still more of these men and their children are graduates of the dozen most highly endowed private schools in the country.

Interactions on corporate and cultural boards also are extensive. Although many Jewish corporate directors are on the boards of corporations founded or taken over by Jewish entrepreneurs, the fact remains that there are important gentile businessmen on those previously all-Jewish boards, just as there are Jewish investment bankers and a handful of other prominent Jewish men and women on the boards of previously all-gentile corporations. Similarly, in the case of the cultural institutions, we have found a considerable degree of interaction between people who are Jewish and people who are not.

Even in the world of clubs, the major exception to our general findings, there is evidence that the barrier is disappearing to some extent, especially in certain cities, such as Chicago, Cincinnati, and Minneapolis. The number of Jews belonging to gentile-founded clubs in Los Angeles, New York, San Francisco, and several other cities is much less impressive, but it seems to be greater than in the early 1960s when Baltzell wrote. As Peter Haas said of the fact that there are now 10 to 15 Jewish members in San Francisco's Pacific Union Club, "It's not that many, but a hell of a lot more than there were." Only in the realm of the country club is the situation virtually unchanged since Baltzell first castigated the Protestant Establishment for its anti-Semitism, and there does not seem to be any indication that those policies will change any time soon. The result will be the persistence of exclusive Jewish country clubs as the most important social institution that serves to remind upper-class gentile and Jew alike that there remain some social barriers between them.

The outcome of these interactions at schools, boards, and (to some extent) clubs should be the kinds of informal interactions that permit friendship and acquaintanceship, along with the most intimate of social interactions, intermarriage. Beyond the evidence from our interviews on friendships formed with gentiles at private schools, cultural institutions, and corporate boards, we know of only one study of acquaintance patterns that provides systematic information on interactions (Domhoff, 1970: 84–87). With the aid of a highly knowledgeable informant, 25 socially elite gentile couples and the same number of socially elite Jewish couples in San Francisco were placed on an alphabetized list. This list was sent to the home addresses of all 50 couples, along with a self-addressed stamped envelope, and they were asked to report how well they knew the other people on the list.

More specifically, respondents were asked to indicate beside each name their degree of acquaintance with the couples by writing "1" (know well); "2" (know casually); "3" (know by reputation only); "4" (do not know). No attempt was made to control whether the husband or wife filled out the questionnaire, on the assumption that any differences in husband and wife acquaintance patterns were too minor to make any restrictions on answering that might reduce the number of questionnaires returned.

The questionnaire took only five minutes to complete, and the responses were entirely anonymous. In what is one of the highest response rates ever recorded for a mail survey, 88 percent of the Jewish families and 76 percent of the gentile families returned the questionnaire within a few days. The replies from both groups were analyzed in terms of an "acquaintance percent" that compared the number of families that rated a "1" or "2" to the total possible ratings. In spite of the exclusionary policies of both the Pacific Union and Bohemian clubs of San Francisco at the time, the acquaintance percent between the two San Francisco groups was 59 percent according to the 22 Jewish respondents and 65 percent according to the 19 gentiles. The similarity of the acquaintance percents as judged from the two groups reinforces the credibility of the finding. As high as these figures are, however, it is nonetheless the case that the acquaintance percents within each of the two groups are even higher: among the Jews in the sample it was 97 percent, among gentiles, 91 percent.

The evidence on intermarriage also is compatible with our thesis, although the number of cases is not great. Studies for the years before the 1970s, when all of the people we interviewed first married, suggest that over 90 percent of all Jews married within their faith. This is similar to what we found in our sample for the new arrivals to the corporate elite. However, the figure was much lower for the longer-term members: only 60 percent. Moreover, the children of both groups, most of whom also married before 1970, were more likely to marry non-Jews than their parents, and once again there were differences between newer and longer-term members. Sixty-eight percent of the married children of the more recent arrivals had married Jews (down over 20 percentage points from their parents' generation), and only 37.5 percent of the children of older-monied members had married Jews (also a drop of over 20 percentage points from the previous generation). Estimates from the late 1970s, as we noted in the first chapter, suggest that nearly 50 percent of all Jews are marrying outside their faith; it seems likely that the figure will be even higher than that for the generation of upper-class Jews who will marry in the 1980s, many of whom will be of third-, fourth-, and even fifth-generation wealth and social status.

Evidence on social interaction and intermarriage approaches the question of class identity by providing information on what seem to be a person's primary reference groups—in this instance, private schools, cultural institutions, and corporations as opposed to synagogues, temples, and secular Jewish organizations. But there is other, more direct evidence that Jewish members of the establishment have their primary identity in class institutions: first, in our scale of Jewish identification; and second, in our interviews. Our study of the degree to which people reveal their Jewishness in their *Who's Who in America* biographies showed that Jewish identification is less for those people who are the most integrated into the major institutions of the corporate and social elites. If people are on corporate boards, or in gentile social clubs, they are less likely to mention any Jewish affiliations, even if they have some. Our interview data paralleled this finding: New arrivals to the corporate elite feel more committed to Jewish organizations and to fundraising for Israel than do those who are long-term members. Sometimes the evidence is even more direct. When we asked one old-line member of the corporate and social elites what being Jewish meant to him, he answered, "It really doesn't mean anything."

However, our view does not claim that Jewish identifications must or will diminish or disappear. It only suggests that class identifications have become of primary importance. Although the numerous conversions by Jews to the high-status Protestant denominations most prevalent in the upper class remain the most dramatic evidence that class wins out at the top over the long run, such conversions are not necessary to our argument, for we believe that people can retain an identification with Jewishness or other ethnic backgrounds while being members of the upper class. To paraphrase an earlier statement by Baltzell, there are middle-class Jews, middle-class Catholics, and middle-class Protestants, but there are Jews, Catholics, and Protestants in the upper class.

The flavor of our conclusion is best stated by Laurence Tisch, perhaps because he is not immersed in the jargon of sociology, or perhaps because he has a unique vantage point as a person worth tens of millions of dollars and active in the Jewish community. "I think that's the tragedy of the Jews. Once they get affluence, and mingle in the non-Jewish world, they think there's something socially more desirable perhaps over there. The big trick is how you keep the Jews as Jews after they get affluent." Laurence Tisch's comment reflects quite well our belief that the Protestant Establishment remains the key reference group in American society. If, as Baltzell claims, the Protestant Establishment is in decline, it is not due to its failure to assimilate Jews.

But is the Protestant Establishment in decline? We think not. A variety of indicators of power show that the strength of the Protestant Establishment remains undiminished despite all the upheavals and challenges of the 1960s and 1970s. The wealth distribution in the United States, which can be viewed as the most stable of power indicators, has not changed for generations, with the top 0.5 percent of the population (the upper class) still owning approximately 22 percent of all privately-held wealth in America and about 50 percent of all corporate wealth (Turner and Starnes, 1976: 38-39; Smith and Franklin, 1974). The income distribution, which is a little more sensitive than the wealth distribution to changes in governmental policies, has been constant since the mid-1940s, with the top 5 percent of income earners receiving 14-16 percent of all money income, and the poor making only slight gains (Turner and Starnes, 1976: 51). The progressiveness of the overall tax burden, despite all the claims by ultra-conservatives and business groups, is not very great due to various loopholes in individual and corporate income taxes. In 1970, for example, the richest tenth of the population paid 27.8 percent of its total income in the form of one tax or another, while the poorest tenth and the second poorest tenth paid only slightly less, 25.8 percent and 24.2 percent, respectively (Okner, 1980).

Liberals, moderates, neo-conservatives, and even populists come and go as presidents, but the number of major business figures appointed to presidential cabinets was as high in 1980 as it was in 1976 and 1960, or even 1900, with only the New Deal cabinet of Franklin D. Roosevelt showing a tendency to include men from the fringes of the corporate community and a greater number of non-business men and women from liberal reform circles (Burch, 1980; 1981; Mintz, 1975). The Senate was known as a "millionaires' club" at the turn of the century when Senators still were picked by state legislatures, but the temporarily rigorous disclosure laws of 1978, now amended, revealed that at least two dozen members in that year were millionaires, about half of whom were Democrats (*Congressional Quarterly*, 1978: 2311). Even the House, expressly designed to be the tribune of the people, included dozens of individuals who were worth several hundred thousand dollars, but exact statements are hard to make because the highest reporting category for each type of property and income was only "over $100,000." Moreover, 128 members filed forms that were incomplete. Nonetheless, it could be determined that an overwhelming number of House members came from occupations in the top 10 percent of the income ladder, a figure that has not changed since studies in 1942, 1956, and 1972 (Zweigenhaft, 1975).

Several indicators, then, show that the power of the Protestant Establishment seems undiminished. Anti-Semitism, as well as prejudice toward other minorities, remains a serious problem within many of its social clubs and, in particular, its country clubs, but other avenues of assimilation and social interaction have kept the establishment intact. We are led to the conclusion that the underlying pressures of the class structure in America, which are often overlooked by social commentators and journalists who focus on issues of race, creed, and ethnicity, remain far more tenacious than even those social scientists most sensitive to establishment power have realized.

Appendix 1

When we checked the two groups in *Who's Who in America*, 1975–76, for their presence or absence in the corporate elite, we found there were more Jewish than non-Jewish foundation trustees on *Fortune*-level boards: 75 of the 219 Jewish trustees sat on one or more boards, but only 54 of the 219 non-Jewish trustees did so ($x^2 = 4.85$, df = 1, p<.05). However, the Jewish directors were less likely to be on the boards of the largest corporations. Although they were on the boards of 13 of the top 100 industrials, the gentiles were on 22 such boards ($x^2 = 2.81$, df = 1, p<.10). When we focused on the ten largest industrials, we found only one Jewish director in the sample, but there were four non-Jewish directors. Or, to consider the pattern of representation from another perspective, 59 percent of the boards with gentile directors were among the top 200 industrials, as compared with only 33 percent of the boards with Jewish directors ($x^2 = 8.80$, df = 1, p<.01).

There also were differences in representation on the boards of the top 50 in banks, diversified financials, life insurance, and retailing. Among the 150 companies in the three financial sectors, there were 22 gentile directors and 13 Jewish directors ($x^2 = 2.62$, df = 1, p<.11). On the other hand, there were 11 Jews and only three non-Jews among the top 50 retails ($x^2 = 5.32$, df = 1, p<.05). Public utility and transportation companies showed no differences.

We traced the new corporate directorships added by the people in these two samples through the next three editions of *Who's Who in America* to 1981, and found no changes in this general pattern. Twelve of the Jewish trustees reported 15 new directorships, and the same number of gentiles added 17 to their biographies, but once again the non-Jews were more likely to join the largest corporations. For example, seven of the ten industrial boards added by the gentiles were in the top 200, but only three of the 13 added by the Jews were at that level ($x^2 = 5.06$, df = 1, p<.05).

Appendix 2

A significant pattern emerged when the age of the various club members was taken into account. There was a clear tendency for the younger club members who are corporate directors to reveal their Jewishness in *Who's Who in America* only through their club memberships or not at all. Whereas only 27 of the corporate directors in these three clubs who were born before 1910 fell into categories #3 and #4, the corresponding figure for those born in 1910 or later was 63 percent ($x^2 = 8.67$, df = 1, p<.01). This was not the pattern for the non-directors: they were no more likely to fall in categories 3 and 4 (in fact 88 of the 158, or 56 percent, fell in categories 1 or 2).

These data were corroborated by a study we did of the 1978 Board of Governors of the American Jewish Committee in which we looked to see if the 49 people who appeared in *Who's Who in America* had included their AJC affiliation in their biographical sketches. We found that 76 percent of those who were not corporate directors included their AJC affiliation, but only 45 percent of those who were corporate directors included it ($x^2 = 3.82$, df = 1, p<.06).

References

Adorno, T. W., E. Frenkel-Brunswik, D. J. Levinson, and R. N. Sanford (1950) *The Authoritarian Personality*. New York: Norton.

Alexander, H. E. (1976) *Financing the 1972 Election*. Lexington, Mass.: D. C. Heath & Co.

Baltzell, E. D. (1958) *Philadelphia Gentlemen: The Making of a National Upper Class*. Glencoe, Ill.: The Free Press.

Baltzell, E. D. (1964) *The Protestant Establishment: Aristocracy and Caste in America*. New York: Vintage Books.

Baltzell, E. D. (1976) "The Protestant Establishment revisited." *American Scholar* 45: 499–518.

Berle, A. A. (1964) "Economic power and the free society," in Andrew Hacker, (ed.) *The Corporation Take-Over*. New York: Harper & Row.

Berman, M. (1979) *Richmond's Jewry*. Charlottesville: University of Virginia Press.

Birmingham, S. (1958) *The Right People*. Boston: Little, Brown.

Birmingham, S. (1967) *Our Crowd: The Great Jewish Families of New York*. New York: Harper & Row.

Birmingham, S. (1971) *The Grandees: America's Sephardic Elite*. New York: Harper & Row.

Bloom, S. (1946) "The saga of America's 'Russian' Jews." *Commentary* 1, 4: 1–7.

Blumberg, P. (1980) *Inequality in an Age of Decline*. New York: Oxford University Press.

Bock, G. E. (1976) The Jewish Schooling of American Jews: A Study of Non-Cognitive Educational Effects. Unpublished Ph.D. dissertation, Harvard University.

Bossard, J. H. S. and E. S. Ball (1948) "Rite of passage—a contemporary study." *Social Forces* (March).

Bugental, J. F. T. and S. L. Zelen (1950) "Investigations into the self-concept." *Journal of Personality* 18: 483–498.

Bunting, D. (1972) "Rise of large American corporations, 1896–1905." Unpublished Ph.D. dissertation, University of Oregon.

Bunting, D. (1976) "Corporate interlocking: Part I—the money trust." *Directors and Boards* 1 (Spring): 6–15.

Bunting, D. (1977) "A new look at interlocks and legislation." *Directors and Boards* 1 (Winter): 39–47.

Burch, P. H., Jr. (1980) *Elites in American History*: Volume III. New York: Holmes & Meier.

Burch, P. H., Jr. (1981) "Reagan's top appointees." Unpublished paper, 1981.

Business Week, Dec. 22, 1975. "Henry Crown: Chicago's ubiquitous capitalist," 30–34.

Business Week, August 11, 1980. "The all-male club: threatened on both sides," 90–91.

Caro, R. A. (1974) *The Power Broker: Robert Moses and the Fall of New York*. New York: Random House.

Centers, R. (1949) *The Psychology of Social Classes*. Princeton, N.J.: Princeton University Press.

Cohen, N. (1972) *Not Free to Desist: The American Jewish Committee, 1906–1966*. Philadelphia: The Jewish Publication Society.

Cohen, S. M. (1979) "The coming shrinkage of American Jewry: a review of recent research," in J. Zimmerman and B. Trainin (eds.) *Renascence or Oblivion: Proceedings of a Conference on Jewish Population, 1978*. New York: Federation of Jewish Philanthropies, 1–25.

Coleman, R. P. and Neugarten, B. L. (1971) *Social Status in the City*. San Francisco: Jossey-Bass, Inc.

Coleman, R. P. and L. Rainwater (1978) *Social Standing in America*. New York: Basic Books.

Cone, E. T. (1973) "The Miss Etta Cones, the Steins and M'sieu Matisse: a memoir," *American Scholar* 42, 3: 441–460.

Cone, S. (Unpublished family history) The Cones of Bavaria.

Congressional Quarterly (1978) "The Wealth of Congress," September 2: 2311.

Converse, P. E., D. Dotson, W. J. Hoag, and W. H. McGee, III (1980) *American Social Attitudes Data Sourcebook, 1947–78*. Cambridge: Harvard University Press.

Cooney, J. (1982) *The Annenbergs*. New York: Simon & Schuster.

Cowan, P. (1967) *The Making of an Un-American*. New York: Viking Press.

Davis, A., B. B. Gardner, and M. R. Gardner (1941) *Deep South*. Chicago: University of Chicago Press.

Davis, J. H. (1979) *The Guggenheims: An American Epic*. New York: Morrow.

Dennis, P. (1980) "Am I a Jew? a radical's search for an answer." *The Nation*, July 12: 44–48.

Dinnerstein, L. and M. D. Palsson (eds.) (1973) *Jews in the South*. Baton Rouge, La.: Louisiana State University Press.

Domhoff, G. W. (1967) *Who Rules America?* Englewood Cliffs, N. J.: Prentice-Hall.

Domhoff, G. W. (1970) *The Higher Circles: The Governing Class in America*. New York: Random House.

Domhoff, G. W. (ed.) (1980) *Power Structure Research*. Beverly Hills: Sage Publications.

Dreier, P. (1981) The position of the press in the American power structure. Unpublished paper.

Dreier, P. and S. Weinberg (1979) "Interlocking Directorates." *Columbia Journalism Review* (November–December): 51–67.

Dye, T. R. (1976) *Who's Running America?* Englewood Cliffs, N.J.: Prentice-Hall.

Dye, T. R. (1979) *Who's Running America? The Carter Years* (Second Edition). Englewood Cliffs, N.J.: Prentice-Hall.

Erikson, E. (1950) *Childhood and Society*. New York: Norton.

Erikson, E. (1958) *Young Man Luther: A Study in Psychoanalysis and History*. New York: Norton.

Erikson, E. (1968) *Identity, Youth and Crisis*. New York: Norton.

Evans, E. (1974) *The Provincials: A Personal History of Jews in the South*. New York: Atheneum.

Feldstein, S. (1978) *The Land That I Show You: Three Centuries of Jewish Life in America*. Garden City, N.Y.: Anchor Press.

Fine, M. and M. Himmelfarb (eds.) (1981) *American Jewish Yearbook*, Volume 81. New York: The American Jewish Committee.

Fortune (1936) "Jews in America." February, XIII, 22.

Fry, C. L. (1933) "The Religious Affiliations of American Leaders." *Scientific Monthly* 36: 241–249.

Gaines, R. (1972) *The Finest Education Money Can Buy*. New York: Simon & Schuster.

Glazer, N. (1979) "American Jews: three conflicts of loyalties," in Seymour Martin Lipset (ed.) *The Third Century: America or a Post-Industrial Society*. Chicago: The University of Chicago Press, 223–242.

Glazer, N. and D. Moynihan (1963) *Beyond the Melting Pot*. Cambridge, Mass.: Harvard University Press.

Glock, C. Y. and R. Stark (1966) *Christian Beliefs and Anti-Semitism*. New York: Harper & Row.

Goffman, E. (1959) *The Presentation of Self in Everyday Life*. New York: Doubleday.

Golden, H. (1943) *For 2¢ Plain*. New York: World Publishing Co.

Golden, H. (1944) *Only in America*. New York: World Publishing Co.

Golden, H. (1955) *Jewish Roots in the Carolinas: A Pattern of American Philo-Semitism*. Greensboro, N.C.: Deal Printing Co.

Gordon, M. (1964) *Assimilation in American Life.* New York: Oxford University Press.

Goulden, J. C. (1973) *The Superlawyers.* New York: Dell Publishing Co.

Gregory, F. W. and I. D. Neu (1952) "The American industrial elite in the 1870's: their social origins," in William Miller (ed.) *Men in Business.* New York: Harper Torchbooks.

Halberstam, D. (1979) *The Powers That Be.* New York: Alfred A. Knopf.

Hamilton, R. (1972) *Class and Politics in the United States.* New York: Wiley & Sons.

Handlin, O. (1954) *Adventure in Freedom: Three Hundred Years of Jewish Life in America.* New York: McGraw-Hill.

Harris, L. (1979) *Merchant Princes: An Intimate History of Jewish Families Who Built Great Department Stores.* New York: Harper & Row.

Herberg, W. (1955) *Protestant-Catholic-Jew.* New York: Doubleday and Co. (Revised Edition, 1960)

Herman, S. (1977) *Jewish Identity: A Social Psychological Perspective.* Beverly Hills, Calif.: Sage Publications.

Herskovitz, M. J. (1974) "Who are the Jews?" in Abraham Chapman (ed.) *Jewish-American Literature: An Anthology.* New York: New American Library, 471–493.

Higham, J. (1975) *Send These To Me: Jews and Other Immigrants in Urban America.* New York: Atheneum.

Himmelfarb, H. (1975) "Measuring Religious Involvement." *Social Forces* 53, 4: 606–618.

Himmelfarb, H. (1980) "The study of American Jewish identification: how it is defined, measured, obtained, sustained and lost." *Journal for the Scientific Study of Religion,* 19, 1: 48–60.

Hoffman, P. (1973) *Lions in the Street.* New York: Saturday Review Press.

Hollingshead, A. B. and F. C. Redlich (1958) *Social Class and Mental Illness: A Community Study.* New York: Wiley.

Hyman, H. (1942) "The psychology of social status." *Archives of Psychology* 38, 269: 1–95.

Isaacs, S. D. (1974) *Jews and American Politics.* New York: Doubleday.

Kahl, J. (1959) *The American Class Structure.* New York: Rinehart.

Kahn, E. J., Jr. (1956) "Director's director." *New Yorker,* September 8 and 15.

Karnow, S. (1974) "Anti-Semitism on the rise?" *New Republic,* December 14: 12–14.

Kennedy, R. (1944) "Single or triple melting-pot? Intermarriage trends in New Haven, 1790–1940." *American Journal of Sociology* 49, 4: 331–339.

Kennedy, R. (1952) "Single or triple melting-pot? Intermarriage in New Haven, 1870–1950." *American Journal of Sociology* 58, 1: 56–59.

Kiester, E., Jr. (1972) *The Case of the Missing Executive.* New York: The American Jewish Committee, Institute of Human Relations.

Korn, B. W. (1973)"Jews and Negro slavery in the Old South, 1789–1865." in L. Dinnerstein and M. D. Palsson (eds.) *Jews in the South*. Baton Rouge, La.: Louisiana State University Press, 89–134.

Kuhn, M. H. and T. S. McPartland (1954) "An empirical investigation of self-attitudes." *American Sociological Review* 19: 68–76.

Lacqueur, W. (1980) *The Terrible Secret*. Boston: Little, Brown.

Lavender, A. (1977) *A Coat of Many Colors: Jewish Subcommunities in the United States*. Westport, Conn.: Greenwood Press.

Lazerwitz, B. (1973) "Religious identification and its ethnic correlates." *Social Forces* 52: 204–220.

Liebman, C. S. (1973) *The Ambivalent American Jew*. Philadelphia: The Jewish Publication Society of America.

Lichter, S. R. and S. Rothman (1982) "Media and Business Elites." *Public Opinion* 4 (5): 42–46; 59–60.

Lipset, S. M. and R. Bendix (1951) "Social class and social structure: a re-examination of data and interpretation: II." *British Journal of Sociology* (October).

Los Angeles Times (1969), "Clubs' barriers thwart careers, study discloses," July 3: A1, A19.

Los Angeles Times (1976), "Pressures mount against discrimination," December 6, 1976: 1, 8ff.

Mace, M. (1971) *Directors: Myth and Reality*. Cambridge, Mass.: Harvard University Press.

Main, J. T. (1965) *The Social Structure of Revolutionary America*. Princeton: Princeton University Press.

Manners, A. (1972) *Poor Cousins*. New York: Coward, McCann and Geoghegan.

Martin, J. B. (1976) *Adlai Stevenson of Illinois*. New York: Doubleday.

Mayer, K. B. and W. Buckley (1969) *Class and Society*, Third Edition. New York: Random House.

McQuaid, K. (1979) "The frustration of corporate revival during the early New Deal." *The Historian*, Vol. XLI (August): 682–704.

Mellow, J. R. (1974) *Charmed Circle: Gertrude Stein and Company*. New York: Praeger.

Miami Herald (1980), "The President's flabby stand on Anti-Semitism," November 3: 2-D.

Mills, C. W. (1956) *The Power Elite*. New York: Oxford University Press.

Mintz, B. (1975) "The President's cabinet, 1897–1972: a contribution to the power structure debate." *Insurgent Sociologist* 5, 3: 131–148.

Mizruchi, M. (1982) *The American Corporate Networks, 1904–1974*. Beverly Hills: Sage.

Newcomer, M. (1955) *The Big Business Executive*. New York: Columbia University Press.

The New York Times (1974a) "Chairman of joint chiefs regrets remarks on Jews," November 14: 1.

The New York Times (1974b) "Off limits," November 14: 46.

Okner, B. A. (1980) "Total U.S. taxes and their effect on the distribution of family income in 1966 and 1970," in H. J. Aaron and M. J. Boskin (eds.), *The Economics of Taxation.* Washington, D.C.: Brookings Institution.

Ostrander, S. A. (1980) "Upper class women: class consciousness as conduct and meaning," in G. W. Domhoff (ed.), *Power Structure Research.* Beverly Hills, Calif.: Sage Publications, 73–96.

Paley, W. (1979) *As It Happened.* Garden City, N.Y.: Doubleday.

Panitz, E. (1963) "The polarity of American Jewish attitudes towards immigration (1870–1891)." *American Jewish Historical Quarterly* (December): 105–118.

Petrusak, F. and S. Steinert (1976) "The Jews of Charleston: some old wine in new bottles." *Jewish Social Studies* 38: 337–346.

Pettigrew, T. F. (1966) "Parallel and distinctive changes in Anti-Semitic and Anti-Negro attitudes, in C. H. Stember (ed.) *Jews in the Mind of America.* New York: Basic Books.

Pollack, B. (1962) *The Collectors: Dr. Claribel and Miss Etta Cone.* New York: Bobbs-Merrill.

Powell, R. M. (1969) *Race, Religion, and the Promotion of the American Executive.* Columbus, Ohio: Ohio State University.

Quinley, H. E. and C. Y. Glock (1979) *Anti- Semitism in America.* New York: The Free Press.

Rayback, J. (1966) *A History of American Labor.* New York: The Free Press.

Reissman, L. (1973) "The New Orleans Jewish community," in L. Dinnerstein and M. D. Palsson (eds.) *Jews in the South.* Baton Rouge, La.: Louisiana State University Press, 288–304.

Reznikoff, C. (1950) *Jews of Charleston: A History of an American Jewish Community.* Philadelphia: Jewish Publication Society of America.

Rischin, M. (1962) *The Promised City.* Cambridge, Mass.: Harvard University Press.

Rollins, J. H. (1973) "Reference identification of youth of differing ethnicity." *Journal of Personality and Social Psychology* 26: 221–231.

Rose, P. I. (1981) *Group Status in America.* New York: Institute of Human Relations of the American Jewish Committee.

Roy, W. G. (1980) American corporate consolidation and the organization of the financial-industrial class segment, 1886–1905. Unpublished paper.

Schlesinger, A. J. (1965) *A Thousand Days.* Boston: Houghton Mifflin Co.

Selznick, G. and S. Steinberg (1969) *The Tenacity of Prejudice: Anti-Semitism in Contemporary America.* New York: Harper & Row.

Sloan, I. J. (1978) *The Jews in America, 1621–1977, A Chronology and Fact Book.* New York: Oceana Publications.

Smith, J. D. and S. D. Franklin (1974) "The concentration of personal wealth, 1922–1969." *American Economic Review* (May) 64, 2: 162–168.

Steel, R. (1980) *Walter Lippman and the American Century.* Boston: Little, Brown & Co.

Steinberg, S. (1974) *The Academic Melting Pot.* New York: McGraw-Hill.

Steinberg, S. (1981) *The Ethnic Myth: Race Ethnicity and Class in America.* New York: Atheneum.

Sturdivant, F. and R. Adler (1976) "Executive origins: still a gray flannel world? *Harvard Business Review* (November–December): 125–133.

Supple, B. (1957) "A business elite: German-Jewish financiers in nineteenth century New York." *Business History Review* 31, 2: 143–178.

Sutker, S. (1958) "The role of social clubs in the Atlanta Jewish community," in Marshall Sklare (ed.) *The Jews: Social Patterns of an American Group.* Glencoe, Ill.: The Free Press.

Synnott, M. G. (1979) *The Half-Opened Door: Discrimination at Harvard, Yale, and Princeton, 1900–1970.* Westport, Conn.: Greenwood Press.

Taylor, J. (1979) "Irving Shapiro, the man." *Delaware Today* (October): 13–17, 44–47.

Trustees of Wealth (1975) Washington, D.C.: Taft Information Services.

Turner, J. H. and C. E. Starnes (1976) *Inequality: Privilege and Poverty in America.* Santa Monica, CA: Goodyear Publishing Co.

U.S. Senate Committee on Governmental Affairs, Subcommittee on Reports, Accounting and Management (1978) *Interlocking directorates among the major U.S. corporations.* Washington, D.C.: U.S. Government Printing Office.

Useem, M. (1978) "The inner group of the American capitalist class." *Social Problems* 25 (February): 225–240.

Useem, M. (1979) "The social organization of the American business elite and participation of corporation directors in the governance of American institutions." *American Sociological Review* 44 (August): 553–572.

Useem, M. (1980) "Which business leaders help govern?" in G. W. Domhoff (ed.) *Power Structure Research.* Beverly Hills, Calif.: Sage Publishing Co.

Vander Zanden, J. W. (1977) *Social Psychology.* New York: Random House.

Verbit, M. (1970) "The components and dimensions of religious behavior: toward a reconceptualization of religiosity," in P. E. Hammond and B. Johnson (eds.) *American Mosaic: Social Patterns of Religion in the U.S.* New York: Random House.

Wall Street Journal (1975) "Breaking the mold: boss-to-be at DuPont is an immigrant's son who climbed the hard way." December 14: 1.

The Washington Post (1974a) "Head of Joint Chiefs criticizes Jewish influence in the U.S." November 13: A1.

The Washington Post (1974b) "Remarks on Jews hit by Ford." November 14: A8.

The Washington Post (1974c) "Brown is 'appalled' by type of reaction." November 26: A5.

Waxman, C. I. (1976) "The centrality of Israel in American Jewish life: a sociological analysis." *Judaism* 2: 175–187.

Waxman, C. I. (1981) "The fourth generation grows up: the contemporary American Jewish community." *The Annals of the American Academy of Political and Social Science* (March): 70–85.

Wechsler, H. S. (1977) *The Qualified Student: A History of Selective College Admission in America*. New York: John Wiley & Sons.

Wise, T. A. (1957) "The bustling house of Lehman." *Fortune* (December): 157–164.

Wise T. A. (1963) "Wherever you look, there's Loeb, Rhoades." *Fortune* (April): 128–132.

Wise, T. A. (1968) "Lazard: in Trinity there is strength." *Fortune* (August): 100–103, 156–165.

Wishnick, W. (1976) *The Witco Story*. New York: The Newcomen Society in North America.

Yankelovich, D. (1973) *The Changing Values on Campus*. New York: Washington Square Press.

Yankelovich, D. (1974) *The New Morality: A Profile of American Youth in the Seventies*. New York: McGraw-Hill.

Zweigenhaft, R. L. (1975) "Who represents America?" *Insurgent Sociologist* 5, 3: 119–130.

Zweigenhaft, R. L. (1978) "The Jews of Greensboro: In or out of the upper class?" *Contemporary Jewry* 4 (2): 60–76.

Zweigenhaft, R. L. (1979) "Two cities in Carolina: A comparative study of Jews in the upper class." *Jewish Social Studies*, XLI: 291–300.

Zweigenhaft, R. L. (1980) "American Jews: in or out of the upper class?", in G. W. Domhoff (ed.) *Power Structure Research*. Beverly Hills, Calif.: Sage Publications, 47–72.

Zweigenhaft, R. L. (1982) "Recent patterns of Jewish representation in the corporate and social elites." *Contemporary Jewry* 6 (1): 36–46.

Index

About the Authors

Richard L. Zweigenhaft is Associate Professor of Psychology at Guilford College in Greensboro, North Carolina. He has published numerous articles in professional psychology and sociology journals, and was educated at Wesleyan University, Columbia University, and the University of California, Santa Cruz. Since joining the faculty at Guilford College in 1974, he has won an Excellence in Teaching award, chaired the psychology department, played basketball for "The Committee Meeting," and (under the name of "Rockaday Johnny") done a weekly show on the college FM radio station.

G. William Domhoff is Professor of Psychology and Sociology at the University of California, Santa Cruz, where he has taught since 1965. He is the author of several books concerning power in America, including *Who Rules America?* (1967), *The Higher Circles* (1970), *The Bohemian Grove and Other Retreats* (1974), and *The Powers That Be* (1979). He received his education at Duke University, Kent State University, and the University of Miami.